SCOTTISH MURDERS

JUDY HAMILTON

WAVERLEY BOOKS

Published 2009 by Waverley Books,
David Dale House, New Lanark, ML11 9DJ, Scotland

ISBN 978 1 902407 83 8

Printed and bound in the UK

CONTENTS

MURDER IN SCOTLAND   5

THE BEAN FAMILY   8

DAVID RIZZIO AND LORD DARNLEY   12

BURKE AND HARE   17

THE DEAD PEDLAR'S TALE: HUGH MCLEOD   24

MADELEINE SMITH   29

JESSIE MCLACHLAN   54

DR PRITCHARD   63

EUGENE MARIE CHANTRELLE   73

JESSIE KING   78

DEATH ON GOATFELL   83

THE MYSTERY OF ARDLAMONT   90

THE MURDER OF MARION GILCHRIST
AND THE TRIALS OF OSCAR SLATER   97

THE DALKEITH POISONER   118

DEATH IN BROUGHTY FERRY   124

PATRICK HIGGINS   132

JOHN DONALD MERRET   135

STANISLAV MYSZKA   145

PETER MANUEL   149

BIBLE JOHN   157

THOMAS ROSS YOUNG   166

THE CASE OF SHEILA GARVIE   171

THE WORLD'S END MURDERS:
CHRISTINE EADIE AND HELEN SCOTT   178

THE ULTIMATE PENALTY   183

INDEX   187

MURDER IN SCOTLAND

Scotland has a bloodstained past. Over the centuries, countless Scots have met a brutal end in battle or in full-scale war. Many hundreds of others have died at the hands of persecutors; so-called witches were hounded from their homes, tortured and put to the death on the most bizarre of charges. The Covenanters were persecuted in the name of the king on account of their religious beliefs. At times the full force of the law itself was almost indistinguishable from murder – the executioner dealt with many poor souls whose crimes would merit no more than a relatively light sentence in modern times. Housebreaking, horse-stealing and petty theft often carried the death penalty. Scotland was indeed a land of rough justice in centuries gone by.

There is always an outcry when crime statistics are published, but in spite of this, it cannot be denied that we live in safer times nowadays. We have a police force working with the benefit of so-phisticated technology to hunt down the few perpetrators of seri-ous, violent crime. We have the law on our side to protect us from persecution. Things are not perfect, but they are very much better than they were.

It is impossible to imagine a time when the streets of Scotland – or any other country – will be crime-free. Human beings are not robots. As much as human beings are capable of good, they are capable of evil.

There is no one answer to the question: 'What makes one person take another's life?' Many murders are committed in the heat of the moment, in outbursts of uncontrollable fury or moments of crazed fear. They are not the result of endless planning and cold, slow, premeditation. When killings like this happen, the murderer may feel the need to kill for no more than a few moments. When the deed is done, the remorse is immediate. These are the killings that make some people say that everyone is capable of murder, given the right (or rather wrong) circumstances.

Some killings are acts of insanity, but the line between psychosis and psychopathic or sociopathic disorder has to be carefully drawn. The psychotic killer suffers from an illness that distorts his mind only for as long as he is ill. The psychotic killer can be treated. The psychotic killer is, in fact, a rare phenomenon. A person suffering from psychosis is much more likely to take his or her own life than the life of another. The behaviour of a psychopath, however, cannot be treated in the same way. A psychopath has a personality disorder and if he feels the need to kill once, he is likely to kill again. It is unlikely that his behaviour will change significantly, in spite of the best efforts of psychiatrists.

Other killings are acts of retribution or revenge, often linked to other crimes. Gang warfare and drug-related crime have both left our streets spattered with the blood of their dead.

Finally, murder is used as a means to an end. The end may be money, sexual gratification, power or freedom. The act of killing may be the end in itself.

This book relates some of the most famous (or infamous) murders in Scotland's history. It cannot begin to tell them all. None of them is pleasant, but all of them are intriguing for different reasons. With the exception of three, the stories of the deaths at Ardlamont and Goatfell, and the case of Madeleine Smith, where the murders were not proven, the stories tell of killings that were certainly premeditated. The story of Oscar Slater tells of a man who was innocent of a crime for which he was convicted, but the crime, whoever did it, had without doubt been carefully planned. The reasons for the killings in the stories that are told here vary considerably and will give the reader an idea of some of the circumstances and some of the motives that can drive a person to murder. Scotland is no exception to any other place in the world. Wherever you go, there will be someone, somewhere, who feels that death is the only answer. And in response to the actions of people like this, we will always ask: 'Why?'

THE BEAN FAMILY

Perhaps the most appalling and grisly tale told of murder in Scotland is that of the Bean family, who held the county of Galloway in the grip of terror in the fifteenth century. The family's catalogue of gruesome crimes continued for some twenty-five years unsolved and many others were to be wrongfully punished for crimes they did not commit before the Beans were finally brought to justice.

At the head of the clan was Sawney Bean. He came from East Lothian, a few miles from Edinburgh, the son of a hedger and ditcher. Any hopes his father might have had for his son to follow him in that profession, humble though it was, or indeed any dreams that he had for his son to make any honest livelihood at all, were swiftly dashed when Sawney ran away from home while still in his teens.

Sawney moved around for a while, finally settling in a remote part of Galloway. There, having joined up with a young woman who shared his desire to live a life free of responsibility or morality, he found himself a cave in which to dwell. Well hidden from the casual passer-by, virtually cut off at high tide, this bleak dwelling place was to suit his purposes perfectly.

Over the course of the next twenty-five years, the Bean family grew in numbers until Sawney and his wife had not only a good number of children but grandchildren as well – nobody knows exactly how many. As the family lived a life in hiding, isolated from general society, it has been assumed that the grandchildren were the products of incestuous relationships.

The family lived entirely by theft, murder and cannibalism. As time passed, people in the surrounding districts grew increasingly alarmed as one story after another of disappearing people was circulated. Locals, visitors and travellers – men, women and children alike – all were vanishing without trace. Alarm in the district spread farther afield, and the government sent men to spy around the area and investigate the crimes. Not only were people disappearing, but sometimes their butchered remains – discarded by the Beans – were found washed up in the shallows around the coast.

The government spies were ferocious rather than thorough in their investigations. Because many of the people who had disappeared had been travelling from one place to another, the most obvious suspects had to be innkeepers. As well as innkeepers, other travellers fell under suspicion. Anxious to get results in their search for the person or persons responsible, the government agents worked with a zeal that bordered on frenzy. They saw to it that several people were detained under suspicion, and some, in spite of insubstantial evidence against them and their own pleas of innocence, were executed. There was, naturally, a feeling of real and terrible fear in the district. When would the disappearances, the killings and the arrests stop? Innkeepers who had not yet felt the strong arm of the law on their shoulders shut up shop and left the area before they, too, came under suspicion. Families, fearing for their own safety, fled to start a new life elsewhere. Travellers with fewer places to stop for the night became more vulnerable: easy prey for the devious, bloodthirsty Bean family.

And devious they were. The Beans had kidnap and murder down to a fine art: so much so that they did not feel the need to confine themselves to killing one person at a time. Their large numbers meant that they had more than enough people to provide sentries to keep watch and assailants to carry out the killing. Their ghastly deeds multiplied unabated and still no one saw anything of the perpetrators. Such was the nerve of the hideous family that some of the government's own men who had been sent to hunt them down fell into their clutches and disappeared.

In the end, it was not through the efforts of the government's men but as a result of one man's fortunate escape from the Beans that their appalling secret was revealed. The man was riding home from a local fair with his wife when they were set upon by a number of the Bean family. The man fought off his assailants bravely but had to witness his poor wife being dragged, screaming, to the ground before having her throat cut. No sooner had she been killed than several Bean women set about disembowelling her and drinking her blood. The man himself would undoubtedly have succumbed as well, for he was outnumbered by the Beans, but a crowd of locals, also returning from the fair, came along the road at that time. The Beans fled from the scene, heading for the safety of their cave.

When the approaching crowd found the man, saw his wife's ravaged corpse and heard what he had to tell them, they saw to it that he was taken to Glasgow immediately, where he had to recount the whole traumatic tale to magistrates.

It was King James himself who led a force of men, some four hundred strong, to Galloway in search of the cannibals. They combed the beaches time and again for signs of human habitation. Finally, at low tide, they found the cave where the Bean family were hiding. It was a shock to find that other human beings should even contemplate living in such a dark and dank hole, but when the searchers advanced into the gloomy passageway of the cave, they found the Bean family, some forty-eight of them in all, surrounded by the booty from their robberies – jewellery, watches, clothing and trinkets – although to what purpose all this finery might serve a family who obviously lived like animals, no one could tell. Horrifying evidence of the family's cannibalism was there for all to see: human parts, hung up to dry or pickled in brine, were all around the cave.

The members of the Bean family were apprehended, struggling furiously with their captors. They were taken to Edinburgh in chains, where, without trial, they were executed. The males were dismembered and left to exsanguinate. The females of the family, after being forced to watch their menfolk bleed to death, were burned at the stake. The treatment that the Beans received in the name of justice was inhuman, but it is perhaps understandable, given the inhuman manner in which they had lived. Their deaths brought an end to what is perhaps the most astonishing and ghastly story of serial killing in the history of Scottish crime.

DAVID RIZZIO AND LORD DARNLEY

The story of the life of Mary Queen of Scots is one marked with tragedy at every turn. Her father, James V of Scotland, died only a few days after she was born. Mary was sent to France when she was barely five years old, betrothed to the young dauphin, whom she married in 1558. But by the age of eighteen, the young queen was a widow. By the age of twenty-five, her life had been changed twice by murder.

In 1559 the French dauphin died. In 1560 Mary of Guise, Mary's mother, who had been acting as regent to the throne in Scotland after the death of James V, also died. Mary returned to Scotland in 1561 to take her place on the throne. The young queen, after arriving in Scotland to a great welcome, soon found that she was not popular with all her subjects. She was a Catholic, and many of the Scottish people, including some of the most powerful of Scotland's nobility, had turned to Protestantism under the influence of John Knox and his followers and consequently saw her as a threat. Mary's own half-brother, Lord James Stewart, Earl of Moray, who had taken control of the country from the death of Mary of Guise until the new queen's return to Scotland, was a Protestant. Mary also had a powerful and determined opponent in Elizabeth I, who was quite determined that Mary should never get the chance to make any sort of claim on the English throne.

At the same time, powerful figures in the Catholic church in Scotland wanted to see Mary firmly established in the country and hoped that Queen Elizabeth I of England, to whose throne Mary was also heir, might be unseated from power. If not, they had to wait and hope that Elizabeth would produce no children of her own, so that Mary could succeed to the throne of England upon Elizabeth's death. With Mary as queen of Scotland and England, the Catholic church would be able to regain all the power that it had lost in recent years. In the struggle between the two sides for power, Mary had precious few true allies on whom she could depend. Her short life must have been a remarkably lonely one.

After she arrived in Scotland, Mary soon realised that she would have to find a husband who, it was to be hoped, would provide her with an heir. In 1565 she remarried – whether or not she married for love is a matter of debate. Her new husband was Henry Stewart, Lord Darnley, also her cousin. Darnley was a Catholic and, like his wife, a threat to the English throne.

Resentment against the young queen was always simmering below the surface. The Protestant lords had considerable power and influence and Mary's position was never secure. Mary's choice of husband was not popular with the nobles, especially Moray.

The marriage to Darnley was not a happy one. Within months of the wedding, Mary had become disenchanted with her new husband. He was outwardly quite a charmer; by all accounts he was an attractive man, accomplished at sport, but there was another less likeable side to him. As a husband, he proved to be uncaring, ill-tempered, selfish and inconsiderate. Mary was unaccustomed to Scottish court life after her years in France and she felt oppressed by the dislike that so many of her subjects so obviously felt for her. If she had hoped to find any solace or support in her marriage to Darnley, she was sorely disappointed.

In the midst of all this misery, one young man in the royal court had caught the attention of the young queen. He was David Rizzio, a young Italian whose skills as a musician were considerable. Mary needed someone to talk to and Rizzio fitted the bill. He was gifted, amusing and, coming from a foreign country, could identify with Mary's sense of estrangement from the Scots. He soon became a close friend and confidant, and she appointed him to the elevated status of being her secretary. Rizzio's position as the queen's 'right-hand man' gave him power, and power made him dangerous.

Opponents of the Scottish queen grew more restive – what sort of influence was this young man having upon her? The threat of Catholic domination seemed to be ever closer. Some of the leading Scottish nobles – the 'rebel lords' – began to plot against Rizzio. They had to find a way to get rid of him.

The conspirators found themselves an unlikely ally in the queen's own husband, Lord Darnley. His motives for joining the conspiracy were different from theirs. Darnley was, quite openly, jealous of Rizzio. Mary seemed to be far too close to him for comfort and there had been rumours that the relationship was more than a friendship. Although Darnley might not have been prepared to be the sort of husband Mary wanted, he certainly did not want her taking up with anyone else. So the scene was set for the ensuing tragedy.

The terrible deed was carried out in the palace of Holyroodhouse in Edinburgh. On the appointed night in March 1566, the conspirators assembled with Darnley. Mary, well into her pregnancy with her first child, was in her chambers with several people, including David Rizzio, in attendance.

The murderers, led by Lord Ruthven, burst in and dragged Rizzio away from his mistress. The other people who had been in the room could only stand by and watch helplessly as the armed intruders, Ruthven, Lindsay, Morton, Douglas, Darnley and others, set upon Rizzio. They stabbed him over and over again: far many more times than was necessary to fulfil their desire to kill him; perhaps this was an indication of the depth of contempt they held for the man. Rizzio's bloodied corpse was then hurled down the stairs to the courtyard.

Mary was left desolate. Although there must have been several people, Mary included, who could have testified against them, the perpetrators of the crime were never brought to justice. Their positions and power were such that their deed went unchallenged and unpunished. Instead, Mary found herself complying with the demands of the murderers that Moray, who had been exiled on account of his treacherous behaviour, be pardoned. And when the alarm was raised after the disturbance in the palace, Mary was not given the chance to cry for help. She herself was threatened with death. The conspirators had, quite literally, got away with murder.

Darnley might have felt avenged by his part in the murder of Rizzio, but the cracks in his relationship with Mary had by now opened into yawning chasms. The two could never be reconciled. Very shortly after Rizzio's death, however, Darnley and Mary had found themselves united in adversity. Darnley had realised that his own safety was at risk from his co-conspirators. Morton, Ruthven et al had been quite prepared to use him in their plot against Rizzio, but they still held Darnley in contempt. Personal characteristics aside, as long as Darnley was married to Mary, the threat to Protestantism in Scotland was doubled. Now the conspirators had Darnley and Mary in their power at Holyrood, they were unlikely to let them go. Mary and Darnley seized the first opportunity to escape and fled to Dunbar, where Mary found enough support for a return to Edinburgh to subdue the followers of the conspirators.

In June 1566, Mary gave birth to her son, the future James VI. When the time came for the child to be christened, Darnley was furious to find that Mary had elected Elizabeth I as godparent. He showed his displeasure by boycotting the christening service. Recently, Mary and Darnley had spent less and less time in each other's company. Now Darnley went to Glasgow, alienating himself further from his young wife.

Mary had been clever in handling the unruly Scots nobility and had found herself a strong ally in the Earl of Bothwell in particular. Her popularity as queen had increased considerably, especially since

15

she had produced a son and heir to the Scottish throne. But Darnley was still deeply unpopular. There were rumours, which reached Mary as well, that Darnley had plans to win the throne of Scotland for himself. Accordingly, there must have been many whose eyes lit up with hope when they heard that the king had fallen ill with what was thought to be smallpox. Dutifully, Mary went to fetch her sick husband and bring him back to Edinburgh. His disease was still at the contagious stage, so it was decided that he should stay at Kirk o' Field, a house on the southern edge of the city.

Darnley's condition improved. His enemies were seething. Something had to be done to get rid of him. A plan was hatched, with Bothwell, Morton and Maitland among the principal schemers, and over the next few days, men started coming and going in the cellars below the house. By the time they had finished, Kirk o' Field was one huge unexploded bomb.

The explosion occurred early in the morning of 10 February 1567 and woke almost the whole city of Edinburgh with its force. Strangely, though, when Darnley's body was found, it was not in amongst the rubble as might have been expected but some distance from the heart of the explosion, with the body of one of his servants beside it. Both men were clearly dead, but their bodies bore no trace of damage from the blast. They had probably been strangled before the house blew up.

Mary Queen of Scots found her world turned upside down by murder for the second time in less than a year. She was once more a widow.

BURKE AND HARE

All murder is horrific. Serial murder strikes particular fear into the hearts of honest citizens and makes them wonder at the mentality of those who carry out such acts. Far worse than this, however, is serial murder that is carried out for profit.

In the late eighteenth century Edinburgh was already established as a centre of medical excellence. The capital city could be justifiably proud of its reputation: many of the country's most eminent doctors had graduated from the university there. Study and research into the mysteries of the human body and its workings were an ongoing process. In order for students and qualified doctors to carry out their anatomical studies effectively, a continuous supply of cadavers was required, but, unfortunately, supply did not always satisfy demand. Doctors were entitled to use the bodies of executed criminals and also those of people who died in prison, but it would appear that these bodies were not enough to satisfy the demands of the inquiring minds of the medical profession.

Thus it was that a lively trade in body-snatching soon grew up in the city. Certain individuals in Scotland's fair capital would visit the graves of the newly dead, where the earth piled on top of the coffin had hardly settled, and remove the bodies from their places of eternal repose. A good price could be fetched for a fresh corpse.

William Burke and William Hare regrettably took their own body business one stage further than this. They made their own corpses.

William Burke came from Ireland to Scotland, first to Glasgow and then to Edinburgh. He was not skilled in any particular trade; instead, he made his living with a succession of manual jobs. When he arrived in Edinburgh, he eventually found work as a labourer. He settled himself in a room at Log's boarding house in Tanner's Close. It was cheap, but hardly cheerful. This was where he first became acquainted with William Hare. The two made an odd couple, by all accounts. Hare was tall and gaunt, with an unmistakably sly, weasel-like countenance. Burke was a good deal shorter than his friend and quite plump. In time, Hare paired up with the owner of the lodging house – Log's widow, Margaret Laird. Burke's 'lady' friend, Helen MacDougal, also took up residence in the house in Tanner's Close. The two women were to play no small part in the horrors that were to follow. They knew full well what the men were up to and gave them every encouragement.

Burke and Hare embarked upon their grisly career quite by chance, as it happened. One of the lodgers in the boarding house fell sick and died, owing a few pounds in rent. The logical thing to do, it seemed to the two men, was to take the body of the lodger to Dr Robert Knox. Dr Knox was a professor of anatomy who lived in Surgeon's Square. It was widely known amongst the criminal fraternity that he would pay well, no questions asked, for cadavers that were brought to him for dissection. The price that Dr Knox would give in return for the corpse would be compensation for the lost rent money. The enterprise was morally wrong, but this was overlooked on account of the fact that, to Burke and Hare, it made sound economical sense.

The two men set to work. The lodger's coffin was prised open, the body was removed, heavy sacks were placed in the coffin to make it seem as if a body was still in it and the coffin was sealed once more, ready for burial. After that, it was a simple matter of waiting until dark before they took the lodger's body to the good doctor and received due payment: more than enough to make up for the rent. They were well pleased.

Shortly after this profitable exercise, another lodger in Tanner's Close fell ill. It was plain that he was going to die and he would make a fine corpse for Dr Knox when the time came. Unfortunately, his decline was too slow for the impatient Burke and Hare. They smothered him quite easily, weak as he was, and the agony of waiting was over in minutes. Another trip to Dr Knox: another few pounds in their pockets.

The body trade was very profitable, but neither Burke nor Hare fancied spending cold nights in the graveyard, armed with spades, always on the lookout for the law. Grave-robbing and body-snatching were risky businesses, and hard work at that. Burke and Hare had discovered a much less strenuous way to supply Dr Knox with bodies. Now all they had to do was to refine a few details to make the same trick work again and again – not just with sick lodgers but with whomsoever they chose. With a little bit of careful planning, it was really very simple.

The first time they tried out their plan, in February 1828, it worked like clockwork. First they selected the victim, Abigail Simpson, an elderly woman. Next they befriended her and took her back to Tanner's Close. Then they got her very drunk. They left her until morning and then topped up her alcohol level until she was barely conscious. After that it was quite a simple matter to suffocate her as she was in no fit state to put up a struggle. That very night, Burke and Hare called upon Dr Knox once more and left the body of Abigail Simpson in his capable hands. (It is said that he made some comments about how fresh the corpse was.) Not counting the cost of the gin that had helped Abigail on her way, Burke and Hare cleared a profit of ten pounds for this exercise.

It was the calculation that went into it, the sheer, cold-blooded impersonal exchange of brutality for gain, that made the crimes of these two men so terrible. They did not care whom, or how many, they killed. For them, the equation was simple: killing = body = money in the coffers. If they were careful enough, they need never be found out. There were plenty of 'invisible' people on the streets of Edinburgh in those days, people who could disappear without anyone even remarking upon their absence.

The next victim after Abigail Simpson was also a woman, a prostitute called Mary Haldane. The same methods were used, with the same results – the money rolled in.

At one point, Burke and Hare tried to double their money. Two young women of ill-repute were lured into their clutches. The two girls, Mary Paterson and Janet Brown, were plied with drink. Mary Paterson gladly obliged by getting exceedingly drunk, but Janet was proving a harder nut to crack. Janet eventually felt so uneasy with the attentions of Burke that she left. Her friend, rendered senseless with alcohol, was considerably less fortunate. Swiftly and efficiently, Mary Paterson was murdered.

Mary Paterson was, however, not one of Edinburgh's invisible people. She was quite a beauty and a familiar figure on the streets of Edinburgh where she plied her trade. There was a difficult moment, apparently, when her body lay on Dr Knox's table, surrounded by eager students. One of the students was sure that he recognised her. Very possibly he did, from some wild night out. The good doctor, however, managed to convince him to the contrary, and before long dissection had rendered the body beyond recognition. Burke and Hare had been careless this time but had still evaded justice.

The number of victims grew; three more, a man and two women, were sent to the great hereafter in swift succession. Then it was the turn of Mary Haldane's daughter to find out first-hand just exactly what had happened to her mother when she vanished from ken. Burke and Hare and their two partners must have revelled in their new-found wealth.

Burke was particularly callous in his search for victims. He took to prowling the streets looking for likely candidates. On one occasion he lured an old beggar woman and her grandson, who was deaf-mute, back to Tanner's Close. The old woman was quickly killed, then, rather than let a potential witness, deaf-mute or not, go free, Burke grabbed the boy and killed him by breaking his back over his knee.

Living and working together, however, was taking its toll on Burke and Hare's friendship. After one particular dispute, when Hare took it upon himself to carry out a business transaction with Dr Knox without Burke's participation, it looked as if their friendship was over. Burke and Helen MacDougal moved out of the house in Tanner's Close. They went to live in a house close to the West Port. Separate living quarters helped to seal up the cracks in the friendship, and it was here that Burke and Hare's working partnership, at least, returned to normal.

The victim this time was Anne MacDougal, Helen's cousin, who lived in Falkirk. Burke and Hare invited her over to Edinburgh for a visit; then, having plied her with drink, disposed of her in the usual manner.

The killing went on for months. Just how many deaths Burke and Hare were responsible for, no one will ever know. Life was cheap on the streets in those days, and there were too many 'nobodies' with too few people to care about what happened to them. All the same, Burke and Hare were getting a little too careless. They had another close shave. One of their last victims was Daft Jamie. Everybody knew him. He was a pleasant fellow, but he was a bit simple and was often the butt of the jokes of local children, who took great delight in teasing him. After he had been killed and sold by Burke and Hare, his body was recognised on Dr Knox's table. His absence was noted on the streets of Edinburgh and he was reported missing. Dr Knox had to be very swift with his dissecting tools.

Then Burke brought home a woman called Mrs Docherty. There were other people in the house at the time and they all had some drinks together. The others left to go and buy some more drink, and Burke and Hare, seizing their chance, killed Mrs Docherty.

When the others got back from their errand, they inquired about the lady who had been there earlier. Burke said that she had left. He seemed jumpy, however, and particularly insistent that no one should go near the bed. Needless to say, at the first opportunity, someone had a quick look around the bed. Underneath, covered in straw, they found the body of Mrs Docherty. Bribes were immediately offered to keep the dreadful deed a secret, but in vain. The police were summoned and Burke, Hare, Margaret Laird and Helen MacDougal were arrested.

Hare was crafty to the end. He and his lady friend managed to save themselves by turning King's evidence and appearing as witnesses for the prosecution in Burke and MacDougal's trial. The trial took place in December 1828, almost one year after the killing spree had begun. Helen MacDougal was set free after a verdict of not proven – she was very lucky, to say the least. Burke was sentenced to death. He was hanged in January 1829, on the twenty-eighth day of the month, in front of a large crowd of jeering spectators. After his death, his body was publicly dissected. Hare, who by rights ought to have met the same end, was hounded out of the city of Edinburgh. He died some years later, blind and impoverished, in London.

Burke's skeleton still hangs in the museum at Surgeon's Hall in Edinburgh. After such a terrible catalogue of crimes, it is quite astonishing that he was the only one to face the full wrath of the law, while Helen, Margaret and Hare all walked free. Even Dr Knox, who cannot have been ignorant of the means that Burke and Hare used to provide him with bodies, came out of it relatively unscathed. He was eventually forced to leave Edinburgh because of public opinion against him, but he escaped legal retribution altogether.

The story of Burke and Hare is well known to people of all ages who live in Edinburgh or who have visited or read about the city. It is a story that has many of the qualities of successful horror fiction, after all. But it should be remembered that Burke and Hare were not the only ones to provide the surgeons of Edinburgh with bodies. There were others who lived around the same time who were willing to desecrate a grave and steal a body to make a quick profit from it.

More significantly, Burke and Hare were not the first to kill in order to provide the medical faculty with a body. On 18 March 1752, two women, named Jean Waldie and Helen Torrance, were hanged in the Grassmarket in Edinburgh for abduction and murder. Their victim was a nine-year-old boy called John Dallas. The two women had killed the child and taken his body to sell to surgeons for anatomical investigations. The price they received for their efforts was nearly three shillings. They were convicted for this one murder only, but it is reasonable to believe that Waldie and Torrance had committed similar crimes prior to this.

THE DEAD PEDLAR'S TALE: HUGH McLEOD

Hugh McLeod came from Assynt. He was the son of a cottar. He had done quite well for himself. He was bright – too bright to become a cottar like his father. He became a teacher instead. His last post was at Loch Broom. We do not know why he gave up teaching, but he did, giving up the schoolhouse that went with his post as well. It was 1830. Hugh McLeod, a man with high aspirations, an eye for the women and expensive tastes by all accounts, was soon broke and heavily in debt.

Murdoch Grant was a pedlar – a travelling man who made his living round various parts of Sutherland selling the goods in the pack that he carried with him. He was hardly a wealthy man, but he made a decent enough living. Naturally, because of the nature of his business, all that he had he carried with him. A pedlar's life may have seemed to be free and easy, but it was not without its problems. There was always the risk of robbery. Lonely tracks and distant places offered plenty of opportunity to the casual thief, and a solitary pedlar, weighed down by his goods, was easy prey. A pedlar had to be on his guard at all times.

When Murdoch Grant met Hugh McLeod in March 1830, his guard must have dropped. He may well have known the former schoolteacher as a customer. Hugh McLeod liked his suits to be made of fine material and he liked to woo his lady friends with trinkets. On the other hand, Murdoch Grant may simply have been seduced by the prospect of a bulging money bag and lulled into a false sense of security by the teacher's silver tongue. When the two men met in Drumbeg, Hugh McLeod offered to buy everything that Murdoch Grant had in his pack, and Murdoch agreed. The two made an amicable agreement to meet the next day and parted in good spirits.

It may seem strange that such an isolated spot was agreed upon for the transaction, but Grant cannot have felt suspicious for he willingly met McLeod on a nearby hillside the next day. The two walked some distance (they were supposed to be heading for the house where Hugh McLeod lived) and finally reached a lochan. Here, Hugh McLeod, armed with a hammer he had brought with him, turned on the pedlar. He struck him to the ground, rifled his pockets and then beat him to death. He heaved the still-warm body of his victim to the edge of the lochan and dragged it as far out into the water as he could. He weighted it down with a large stone, but it was still visible to anyone who might look into the water.

McLeod was to admit much later in his confession to the crime that he simply lacked the courage to retrieve the body and bury it elsewhere. He took several small items from the pedlar's pack, but took the pack and all the bulkier, heavier goods that Murdoch had carried in it to a nearby lochan and concealed the whole lot underwater there.

Murdoch Grant had been a familiar figure in the district and it was not long before he was missed. It took four weeks, however, before the body was found in the lochan, spotted by an eagle-eyed passer-by. The alarm was raised and a sizeable crowd gathered to watch as the dead man was pulled out onto the shore by local inhabitants. The body was still recognisable as that of the missing travelling salesman. It was debatable whether the pedlar had fallen in and hit his head and then drowned, or whether he had been killed. His pack – which he had never been without – was missing. Thus, even to those humble lay persons who were present, it seemed much more likely that murder had been committed, with robbery as the motive. But Hugh McLeod, the schoolmaster, the one learned man amongst them, was adamant. According to him, the whole sad affair must have been an accident.

It had once been customary in Scotland to subject all possible suspects of foul play in a case such as this to a procedure known as 'ordeal by touch'. Suspects were brought to the body of a murder victim and asked to touch it. According to belief, blood would issue from the body of the victim when it was touched by the murderer. Most of those who were present when the body of Murdoch Grant was pulled from the lochan were happy to comply with tradition in the absence of legal authorities: if Grant had been killed deliberately, touching his body would prove their own innocence. Hugh McLeod, needless to say, was having none of it. This was an old-fashioned superstition, he blustered, based on nothing but pure fancy. He wanted nothing to do with it. The other people present were convinced by his attitude of disdain and felt a little foolish for indulging in superstitious nonsense. We know, better than they did, the real reason why McLeod would not submit to the ordeal by touch. He must have believed in it – and he had something to fear from it.

McLeod was equally persuasive when it came to forcing his personality upon the investigating authorities. He knew that he had to convince them not to take any further action. Fortunately, it had conveniently fallen upon McLeod to be the one to inform the authorities of the discovery in the lochan, and by the time he had finished talking to the local magistrates, they too were quite convinced that Murdoch Grant's death had been no more than a tragic accident. He had fallen into the water and hit his head. There was no need to proceed with the matter any further. Grant was buried shortly afterwards and Hugh McLeod, no longer tortured by the sight of his victim's body in the clear waters of the lochan, could sleep a little easier.

His freedom was short-lived, however. Within days, Murdoch

Grant's brother, Robert, was on the trail. He knew his brother had been murdered. He set out to look for justice. Upon his insistence, the body of Murdoch was disinterred and re-examined. This revealed little more than had already been seen, but as this second examination was carried out by people better qualified for such a job, the interpretation of the evidence was different. The question as to whether Grant had been attacked or had fallen into the lochan, hit his head and drowned, was now answered authoritatively. Hugh McLeod, of course, continued to insist that it had been an accidental death. The examining doctors, however, felt that the marks on Murdoch's head were much more consistent with blows from a blunt instrument, such as a hammer . . . .

Robert Grant was equally determined that his brother had been killed deliberately and began looking for clues that would reveal the killer's identity. He set about trying to find out what had happened to his brother's pack and to the money that must have been on his person. A search of the district was carried out, but in vain. The only breakthrough in finding any of Murdoch Grant's possessions came with the help of a known seer, Kenneth Fraser, also known as Kenneth the dreamer. Kenneth said that he had seen the murder in a dream. The pedlar's pack was concealed beneath a cairn made of stones, he said. Kenneth described the place where the cairn was with astonishing accuracy. The searchers found the cairn and although there was no sign of the pedlar's pack, some of Murdoch Grant's personal possessions still lay beneath the stones that had been piled there.

Meanwhile, the investigation had rounded on Hugh McLeod. He had always been a big spender, but now he was spending more than ever. He seemed to be in possession of amounts of money that were all out of proportion to anything he might have earned as a schoolmaster. It was not long before Hugh McLeod was arrested and incarcerated in Dornoch Jail, charged with the murder of Murdoch Grant.

The schoolmaster, who had professed an educated disdain for superstition when he stood beside the body of his victim, found himself indulging in it one more time. During his stay in Dornoch Jail, he dreamt that he met his father in a churchyard. His father was standing beside an open grave and an open coffin. His father announced to the terrified Hugh that this was his grave. Hugh would be allowed twelve more months, but after that time he would have to lie down in it. It was September 1830. Hugh believed all that he had dreamt.

The trial should have begun that month in Inverness, but it was postponed until the following spring. Then followed a further postponement, and Hugh McLeod was left to ponder his fate for another five months. The trial took place in Inverness, lasting from 26 September until 27 September – a full twenty-four hours. Hugh McLeod was found guilty, by a unanimous verdict, of the murder of Murdoch Grant. When sentence of death was passed, McLeod loudly protested his innocence, but in the days leading up to his death, his attitude changed. He confessed to everything and gave every sign that he was a different man, such was his display of piety. Twelve months had passed since he had seen his father in the dream in Dornoch prison.

On 24 October Hugh McLeod walked to the gallows in Inverness and awaited his death singing psalms loudly in Gaelic. When the rope jerked, his singing was silenced forever.

MADELEINE SMITH

In April 1855 Madeleine Smith, one of Glasgow's most desirable young women, put pen to paper to compose the first letter in a correspondence that was to cause the greatest scandal in Glasgow society of its time.

> My dear Emile,
> I do not feel as if I were writing you for the first time. Though our intercourse has been very short, yet we have become as familiar friends. May we long continue so. And ere long may you be a friend of Papa's is my most earnest desire. We feel it rather dull here after the excitement of a town's life. But then we have much more time to devote to study and improvement. I often wish you were near us. We could take such charming walks. One enjoys walking with a pleasant companion, and where could we find one equal to yourself?

Madeleine was eighteen years old, the daughter of George Smith, a Glasgow architect of considerable wealth and standing. She had recently returned to the city after completing her education in England at a school in Clapton. Upon her return, she soon immersed herself in high society in Glasgow, attending any social occasion that was worth attending and entertaining the elite of the city at her father's house. She was an attractive young woman: small and pleasantly rounded, with dark eyes and a pretty, animated face. She would have no shortage of suitors.

The man who had caught Madeleine's attention was, however, an unlikely candidate for her hand in marriage. Pierre Emile

L'Angelier was a humble clerk – hardly a suitable match for a young woman of Madeleine Smith's position. He lived in sparse lodgings while she lived in a large house in the centre of the city. She was not yet twenty. He was ten years older.

Pierre Emile L'Angelier had high aspirations, however. He hoped to marry well. To this end, he was quite prepared to play upon all that was most intriguing about his French origins. He liked to give the impression that he was very well connected in the country of his father's birth (L'Angelier himself was born in Jersey) and, in spite of his impecunious situation, he liked to cut a dash in the streets of Glasgow, taking meticulous care with his dress and personal appearance. Several people who had met him socially or worked with him were later to say that he was quite a vain man.

Given his desire to marry a young woman of social standing, it was inevitable that L'Angelier would know who Madeleine Smith was. Very cleverly, he engineered an opportunity to be introduced to her. Madeleine Smith and her sister Bessie were in the habit of taking walks in the afternoon along Sauchiehall Street. L'Angelier had seen them there many times himself. It would have been most improper for him to have approached the ladies independently, but, fortunately, another man who worked at Huggins and Co. with L'Angelier knew the Smith family. L'Angelier persuaded his colleague, Robert Baird, to parade up and down Sauchiehall Street with him until they 'chanced' upon Madeleine and her sister. Baird introduced L'Angelier. Gradually, as propriety demanded, L'Angelier and Madeleine became better acquainted. Further 'chance' meetings in Sauchiehall Street were engineered by both parties, and soon Madeleine and L'Angelier had become embroiled in a relationship that went far beyond that of polite acquaintance.

The relationship had to remain a secret. There was no doubt in Madeleine's mind that her father would not approve of her friendship with L'Angelier, but she was completely fascinated with the dapper foreigner. He was clever, he was interesting, and he was forbidden fruit. Madeleine needed no persuasion. She was hooked. Moreover, she encouraged the attentions of L'Angelier with a lack of modesty that was quite remarkable for Victorian times.

When it was brought to George Smith's attention that his daughter Madeleine had been walking in town with L'Angelier, he was none too pleased. Madeleine wrote to L'Angelier again, telling him that she could no longer see him. Whether this was what she really meant or whether the letter was written to appease her father, Madeleine did not stop seeing L'Angelier. Friendship had blossomed into romance, and now the two contrived to meet in secret at Madeleine's home or at the home of an elderly friend of L'Angelier's, Miss Mary Perry. When they could not see each other, the two continued to correspond by letters that were passed to each other with the help of one of the servants in the Smith household.

Needless to say, Madeleine's father found out that she was still seeing L'Angelier. He ordered her once more, this time more forcefully, to put an end to the friendship. She wrote of her disappointment to Miss Perry, using the name that she had now adopted in her correspondence with L'Angelier:

> Emile will tell you I have bid him adieu. My papa would not give his consent, so I am in duty bound to obey him. Comfort dear Emile. It is a heavy blow to us both. I had hoped some day to have been happy with him, but alas it was not intended. We were doomed to be disappointed. . . . Think my conduct not unkind. I have a father to please, and a kind father too. Farewell, dear Miss Perry, and with much love believe me, yours most sincerely,
>
> Mimi

In spite of all these fine words, however, Madeleine continued to see L'Angelier behind her father's back. The Smith family had a country house, Rowaleyn, at Rhu, and even there Madeleine was able to arrange meetings with her sweetheart. Summer passed, then autumn. When winter came, the two lovers had the flames of their passion to keep them warm. In between meetings, they continued to write to each other. Madeleine's letters to L'Angelier, carefully preserved by him, displayed a frankness that was to cause a sensation when they were read out in court eighteen months later. There was now talk of a secret marriage being arranged in Edinburgh, and Madeleine referred to L'Angelier as 'my own darling husband'. In addition to this, it was clear that the relationship was by now getting dangerously physical:

> I did not expect the pleasure of seeing you last evening, of being fondled by you, dear, dear Emile . . .

Was Madeleine sincere when she professed her desire to wed L'Angelier, or was she leading him on in this respect in order to sustain the thrill of a wickedly clandestine liaison? Certainly, letters exchanged in the following few months could easily give the impression that it was Madeleine who took the lead in the physical side of their relationship, while L'Angelier showed more concern for morality and constraint. But by the early summer of 1856, it seems that L'Angelier had finally given in to his own and Madeleine's passion. The Smith family were once more at Rowaleyn, the country house they owned at Rhu. The rural surroundings helped Madeleine and L'Angelier considerably. It was easier to find a secluded place to meet without fear of interruption. The following extracts from a letter written by Madeleine reveal her feelings about the consummation of their love:

> . . . It is truly a pleasure to see you, my Emile. Beloved, if we did wrong last night it was in the excitement of our love. Yes, beloved, I did truly love you with my soul. I was happy, it was a pleasure to be with you. Oh if we could have remained, never more to have parted . . .

. . . You must be very disappointed with me. I wonder you like me in the least. But I trust and pray the day may come when you like me better . . .

. . . I did not bleed in the least last night – but I had a good deal of pain during the night. Tell me, pet, were you angry at me for allowing you to do what you did – was it very bad of me? We should, I suppose, have waited till we were married. I shall always remember last night . . .

Madeleine seemed more concerned for L'Angelier's approval than anything else. It is not her own regrets that worry her but rather those that L'Angelier might have.

L'Angelier's letter to Madeleine in reply shows that she was right to be concerned about what he thought. It is interesting how he insinuates that she is the one to blame for their mutual loss of self-control:

. . . Since I saw you I have been wretchedly sad. Would to God we had not met that night – I would have been happier. I am sad at what we did. I regret it very much. Why, Mimi, did you give way after your promises? My pet, it is such a pity. Think of the consequences if I were never to marry you. What reproaches I should have, Mimi. I shall never be happy again. If I ever meet you again, love, it must be as at first. I will never repeat what I did until we are regularly married . . .

Madeleine might have been keeping L'Angelier hanging on with her promises of marriage, but now perhaps L'Angelier had the upper hand: 'Think of the consequences if I were never to marry you.' Who was manipulating whom?

Madeleine wrote nearly two hundred letters to L'Angelier. He kept them all. We would know nothing of his replies to her were it not for the fact that he also kept draft copies of some of them.

His motives for preserving the evidence of their correspondence so meticulously have often been called into question. Did he keep Madeleine's letters as keepsakes of their romance or as a lever, a tool in his machinations to get her to marry him? He had already mentioned the possibility of going abroad to try to improve his financial situation. He now tells Madeleine that, of course, if they were to be married, he would not go. His letter continues, a strange mixture of concern and reproach:

> . . . I do not understand, my pet, your not bleeding, for every woman having her virginity must bleed. You must have done so some other time. Try to remember if you never hurt yourself in washing, etc. I am sorry you felt pain. I hope you are better. I trust, dearest, you will not be with child – be sure and tell me immediately you are ill next time, and if at your regular period. I was not angry at your allowing me, Mimi, but I am sad it happened. You had no resolution. We should indeed have waited till we were married, Mimi. It was very bad indeed. I shall look with regret on that night. No, nothing except our marriage will efface it from my memory . . .

L'Angelier had always been a jealous suitor. He disapproved of Madeleine's attendance at balls and other social occasions where he could not be present and where she might be subject to the attentions of other men. He hated to think that she might be flirting in his absence. A few months after the anguished exchange of letters above, it became clear to L'Angelier that there might be real competition for Madeleine; competition in the form of one William Minnoch, a much better prospect as far as Madeleine's family were concerned. William Minnoch was wealthy, a partner in a firm of cotton spinners. Whilst reassuring L'Angelier that her heart remained true to him and him alone, Madeleine was keeping company with Minnoch more and more frequently. Soon, she had two sweethearts – one confined to darkness and stolen moments, the other free to spend time with her quite openly and with her father's approval.

L'Angelier had been under the impression that Madeleine would marry him, no matter what the consequences might be and regardless of her father's feelings on the matter. She had given him the impression that her mother knew about the relationship and it was only a matter of time before Madeleine told her father as well. He had believed they would be married in September 1856. But as events progressed, this seemed an increasingly unlikely prospect.

It is more than likely that Madeleine never intended to keep all her promises to become L'Angelier's wife. Her entire family remained unaware of the fact that she had defied her father and continued the liaison with L'Angelier. She had never made any attempt to bring the affair out into the open, let alone beg her father to accept L'Angelier as her future husband. In all probability, she never intended to tell them anything.

Madeleine's family moved house from India Street to a property in Blythswood Square. The flat above theirs was occupied by none other than William Minnoch. As William Minnoch grew closer to Madeleine, so she sought to put some distance between herself and L'Angelier:

. . . I promised to marry you knowing I would never have my father's consent. I would be obliged to marry you in a clandestine way. I knew you were poor. All these I did not mind. I trust we have days of happiness before us – but God knows we have days of misery too. Emile, my own, my ever dear husband, I have suffered much on your account from my family. They have laughed at my love for you – they taunted me regarding you. I was watched all last winter. I was not allowed out by myself for fear I should meet you – but if I can I shall cheat them this winter. I shall avoid you at first, and that may cause them to allow me out myself. I shall write to you as often as I can – but it cannot be three times a week as it has been . . .

It is clear that Madeleine was trying to impress upon L'Angelier that their marriage could never be acceptable in her father's eyes and thus could never be acceptable in the social circles in which Madeleine moved. L'Angelier would not reach the status to which he aspired. So why did Madeleine not put an end to the affair, there and then? Was she still enjoying the intrigue or was she frightened of the consequences of severing all ties with L'Angelier? Certainly, he could damage her reputation irrevocably if he chose so to do.

For reasons that will never be known for sure, Madeleine kept up her correspondence with L'Angelier and continued to see him in stolen moments at her bedroom window in the basement of the house in Blythswood Square. L'Angelier expressed his anger and frustration that Madeleine was spending time quite openly with Mr Minnoch. She appeased him with sweet nothings and cups of cocoa.

It was all getting very tiresome for Madeleine. Minnoch was clearly intending to propose to her in the near future. Good sense will have dictated to Madeleine that acceptance was her only option. Minnoch was good marriage material and, besides, she liked him. But she still had L'Angelier to deal with. Her letters grew less affectionate in tone as she sought to put him off his pursuit of her. The best outcome would be for him to lose interest in her and put an end to the relationship himself. This is probably the outcome that Madeleine sought. But L'Angelier was proving much harder to shake off than she had hoped. Her tactics seemed to change from one letter to another. Some letters would make mention of Mr Minnoch and her growing fondness for him. Others professed her continued love for L'Angelier, emphasising at the same time the hopelessness of their predicament:

. . . I did tell you, at one time, that I did not like William Minnoch, but he was so pleasant that he quite raised himself in my estimation. I wrote to his sisters to see if they would come and visit us next week, also him, but they cannot . . .

. . . I weep now, Emile, to think of our fate. If we could only get married, and all would be well. But alas, I see no chance, no chance of happiness for me.

In January 1857, Minnoch proposed. Madeleine accepted. She continued in her efforts to put L'Angelier off without actually admitting that she was now betrothed to another. Finally, her attitude provoked L'Angelier into sending one of her letters back. Her response to this was quite emphatic:

When you are not pleased with the letters I send you, then our correspondence shall be at an end, and as there is coolness on both sides our engagement had better be broken . . .

. . . Altogether I think owing to coolness and indifference (nothing else) that we had better for the future consider ourselves as strangers. I trust to your honour as a gentleman that you will not reveal anything that may have passed between us. I shall feel obliged by your bringing me my letters and likeness on Thursday evening . . .

. . . On Friday night I shall send you all your letters, likeness, etc.

. . . For some time back you must have noticed a coolness in my notes. My love for you has ceased, and that is why I was cool. I did once love you truly, fondly, but for some time back I have lost much of that love . . .

. . . There is no other reason for my conduct, and I think it is fair to let you know this. I might have gone on and become your wife but I could not have loved you as I ought. My conduct you will condemn, but I did, at one time, love you with heart and soul. It has cost me much to tell you this – sleepless nights – but it is necessary you should know . . .

. . . I know you will never injure the character of one you so fondly loved. No, Emile, I know you have honour and are a gentleman. What has passed you will not mention. I know, when I ask you that, you will comply. Adieu . . .

Did dearest Emile detect a hint of desperation in her tone? Almost certainly. Did he return Madeleine's letters to her? Of course he did not. Instead, he announced that he had no alternative but to reveal all to Madeleine's father.

Madeleine was in real trouble now. She begged L'Angelier to reconsider. She admitted to him that she had never told her family of their 'engagement', but still denied that her heart had been won by any other. She pleaded with L'Angelier to preserve her reputation and sought his pity – if her father found out what had happened between them, she would be cast out from the family. She even hinted at suicide in her desperation: 'I feel as if death indeed would be sweet.'

L'Angelier relented. He met with Madeleine, and while she managed to avert the disaster of his betrayal, it was L'Angelier who emerged the victor. The relationship was back on track with L'Angelier firmly in command.

The scene was now set for the tragedy to follow – doomed love, reputations at stake, a hint of blackmail, a touch of desperation. It must have been obvious to both Madeleine and L'Angelier that things could not go on as they had done for much longer. One of them had to do something. And something was done, but the question that was left and still remains unanswered is 'Who did it?'

Around the time of Madeleine's desperate begging letter to L'Angelier, the Frenchman started a daily journal, and there is no evidence to suggest that he kept one at any time before then. The first entry was made on 11 February 1857:

Dined at Mr Mitchell's – Saw Madeleine at 12 p.m. in Christina Haggart's room. (Christina Haggart was a servant in the Smith household who had been very helpful to Madeleine and L'Angelier since the beginning of their relationship.)

On 13 February another reference to Madeleine is made:

Saw Mr Phillpot. Mimi. Dined at 144 Renfrew Street. (144 Renfrew Street was the address of Mary Perry.)

The next few entries in the diary were no more than brief records of daily trivia, but on 19 February things were obviously beginning to go wrong:

Saw Mimi a few moments. Was very ill during the night.

On Friday 20 February, L'Angelier recorded another meeting with Madeleine in his journal. The entry for the following day is brief, but to the point:

Don't feel well. Went to T. F. Kennedy's.

On Sunday 22 February, another meeting with Madeleine is noted:

Saw Mimi in Drawing Room. Promised me French bible. Taken very ill.

A pattern was clearly beginning to emerge – L'Angelier saw Madeleine, then L'Angelier became unwell. The records in L'Angelier's diary were backed up by the details that Mrs Jenkins, his landlady, was later able to supply to the police. She had found

L'Angelier unwell one morning when she called upon him. He had been vomiting green-coloured fluid which the landlady took to be bile.

On 23 February, Mrs Jenkins was called to L'Angelier's room again. He was cold, thirsty and in pain. Once again, he was vomiting a bile-like fluid. Mrs Jenkins called the doctor, who prescribed some medication.

Interestingly, at around the same time as L'Angelier began to feel ill, Madeleine made a short trip to the chemist's, Murdoch Brothers, in Sauchiehall Street. There she bought one ounce of arsenic, which was mixed with soot. She told the chemist that she wanted the powder for the Smiths' country house.

On 2 March L'Angelier visited Miss Perry, and she noticed that he was unwell. He told her about the sickness he had been suffering from and said to her that he had become unwell after drinking chocolate.

One week later, he visited Miss Perry again. Once again, he made the connection between a cup of hot chocolate and the sickness that had felled him so suddenly. This time, he told Miss Perry that it was Madeleine who had given him the chocolate. One particular remark that he passed about his beloved seems ominous in retrospect:

It is a perfect fascination, my attachment to that girl. *If she were to poison me I would forgive her.*

Meanwhile, Madeleine and L'Angelier were still writing to each other. Madeleine was due to leave for Bridge of Allan in the near future. It was there, at the spa town three miles north of Stirling, that William Minnoch and she intended to announce the date of their forthcoming marriage. L'Angelier must have announced his intention to pay a visit to Madeleine in Bridge of Allan, but this she could not countenance. Minnoch and L'Angelier must never meet. So she urged him by post to go to England for the sake of his health – perhaps to the Isle of Wight – but to stay away, please stay away from Stirling:

> . . . as it is a nasty dirty little town.

L'Angelier was clearly very suspicious and very jealous. He knew perfectly well that in all probability, Minnoch and Madeleine would be meeting up in Bridge of Allan. His letter implored her for a truthful account of her relationship with Mr Minnoch and indicated that he would settle this time for nothing less than the whole truth. Madeleine wrote back to stall him. No, of course there was nothing of any importance going on between her and Mr Minnoch. Please could L'Angelier wait in Glasgow for her return and not go to Bridge of Allan. Perhaps a visit to the spa there would benefit his health, but it would be better for him to wait until Madeleine's stay there was over.

When she had written to L'Angelier, Madeleine continued with her arrangements for the wedding to William Minnoch. She met up with an old school-friend, Mary Jane Buchanan, to discuss the wedding date. On their way back home, Madeleine asked her friend to come into the chemist's shop with her. This was not the same chemist as she had visited before. It was Currie's, at Charing Cross. Madeleine bought herself sixpence-worth of arsenic from Currie's, saying as she signed the register that she wanted it to kill rats in the cellar at home. This time, the arsenic powder that she bought was mixed with indigo.

Her shopping was done, her business had been attended to. Now Madeleine could set off for Bridge of Allan. The trip went very well. William Minnoch visited the Smiths as planned and a date was officially set for the wedding. In June, Madeleine was to become Mrs Minnoch.

And still L'Angelier was none the wiser. He did not go to Bridge of Allan while Madeleine was there. He did take a trip through to Edinburgh, however, and called upon Miss Perry's sister, Mrs Towers, and her husband, who lived at Portobello. During his visit, he spoke at great length about the problems he had been having with his health. Once again, he spoke in some detail about his recent illness. He told Mr and Mrs Towers that he had drunk coffee and chocolate and that they had made him ill. In fact, he told them, he believed the drinks had been poisoned.

Madeleine returned to Glasgow on 17 March. On 18 March, she visited Currie's the chemists again and bought another ounce of arsenic. When she was asked for what purpose she wanted the poison, she said again that it was for killing rats. The next day, she wrote a letter to L'Angelier, but he did not get it in time to arrange a meeting with her. He had left for Bridge of Allan on the day of her writing and the letter had to be sent on to him there. When it reached him, on 20 March, he wrote to Mary Perry and spoke of his disappointment at missing Madeleine:

. . . I should have come to see someone last night but the letter came too late so we are both disappointed . . .
. . . I shall be here till Wednesday.

As it happened, L'Angelier did not stay in Bridge of Allan until the Wednesday. Instead, he returned on the evening of Sunday 22 March. He had received another letter from Madeleine, which had been sent on by Mrs Jenkins, his landlady. When he reached Glasgow, he told Mrs Jenkins that the letter was the reason for his early return. He stayed long enough at his lodgings to have a bite to eat and change his clothes, and then he left at about nine o'clock in the evening.

What happened in the next few hours is a mystery. At about half past two in the morning, Mrs Jenkins was rudely awakened when L'Angelier arrived back in a state of considerable distress. He was cold, he said, and had terrible pains in his stomach. The kindly Mrs Jenkins tucked him up with hot-water bottles in bed. Some time later, when L'Angelier's condition deteriorated, she called upon a doctor for his advice. The doctor prescribed some treatment, which L'Angelier refused. He continued to get worse, and at around seven in the morning, Mrs Jenkins went out and brought the doctor back to see L'Angelier for himself. The doctor applied a poultice but, apart from voicing a suspicion that L'Angelier had been drinking, was unable to determine what was wrong with him.

L'Angelier continued to deteriorate in the next two hours. Shortly after nine o'clock, Mrs Jenkins sent her son to fetch Miss Perry, with L'Angelier's consent. He was obviously seriously ill. When Miss Perry arrived at the house, she found the doctor in attendance. L'Angelier was dead.

The doctor in attendance did not know L'Angelier, so L'Angelier's own doctor was called to give his opinion on the matter. L'Angelier's employers, Huggins and Co., were informed and William Stevenson from the company came round. Monsieur Thuau, a fellow lodger at Mrs Jenkins' house, was also present. Together, they started to look through L'Angelier's personal belongings. All his letters from Madeleine were there; one of them was still in a pocket in the clothes that L'Angelier had been wearing the night before. It was the last letter he had received from Madeleine, the one that had brought him back early from Bridge of Allan:

. . . Why my beloved did you not come to me? Oh beloved are you ill? Come to me, my sweet one. I waited and waited for you but you came not. I shall wait again tomorrow night same hour and arrangement. Do come, sweet love, my own dear love of a sweetheart. Come, beloved, and clasp me to your heart. Come and we shall be happy. A kiss fond love. Adieu with tender embraces ever believe me to be your own ever dear fond Mimi.

Things moved on rapidly from there. Miss Perry went round to the Smith family house, not to see Madeleine but to see Mrs Smith to tell her of L'Angelier's death. Monsieur Auguste de Mean from the French consulate visited Mr Smith and told him of the letters that L'Angelier had received from Madeleine. While Mr and Mrs Smith were left reeling from the revelations about their daughter, the body of Pierre Emile L'Angelier was being taken away for post-mortem examination.

Mr and Mrs Smith both retired to bed. It was clearly all too much for both of them. They were to remain indisposed for some time, in fact keeping themselves well out of the public gaze right through the period of their daughter's arrest and subsequent trial.

Madeleine, on the other hand, was outwardly quite calm at this point. L'Angelier had died on the morning of Monday 23 March. Madeleine had a social engagement on the Wednesday night. She went out for dinner with William Minnoch, and everything seemed quite normal to her fiancé.

The next morning, however, when William Minnoch called at the Smith house, Madeleine had gone. Her father did not enlighten Minnoch as to the exact reasons for Madeleine's sudden departure but did mention something about an old love affair.

Madeleine was probably in a state of some panic by now. The previous afternoon, she had had a visit from Monsieur de Mean. He wanted to know how L'Angelier had spent the hours between nine in the evening on the night before his death and two-thirty in the morning when he had returned, so unwell. He knew of Madeleine's last letter to L'Angelier and believed that the two must have met that night. He urged Madeleine to tell the truth. This visit must have been preying upon Madeleine's mind all night as she dined with William Minnoch. The next morning, she had packed up and left.

Very gallantly, Minnoch set off in hot pursuit. His instinct told him that Madeleine would probably head for the family house at

Rhu, and he was correct. He caught up with her and urged her to come home. He was very supportive. At this stage, however, he was still unaware of the seriousness of the situation.

L'Angelier's body, which had been buried on 26 March, was exhumed on 31 March. The post-mortem had revealed evidence of poisoning and further examination of the corpse was necessary. On the same day, Madeleine Smith was arrested and charged with the murder of Pierre Emile L'Angelier. The rumours that had been flying around respectable society in Glasgow gathered into a storm cloud of scandal.

Madeleine's statement on the day of her arrest made the following points:

1   She admitted that she had known L'Angelier for two years and that the two had met on several occasions.
2   She stated that she had not seen L'Angelier for three weeks or so. They had last met at her bedroom window, three weeks before his death, at about half-past ten at night.
3   She said that they had been in the habit of writing notes to each other. She had written to him on Friday 20 March and had expected him to come and see her on Saturday the 21st. He had not appeared. She had then waited for him to come to her window on the Sunday night, but he had not come and she had gone to bed at eleven o'clock and remained there until eight or nine the following morning.
4   She admitted that she had made plans for marriage with L'Angelier, originally for the previous September and more recently for this March. They had spoken of finding furnished lodgings, but the plans had got no further than that.
5   L'Angelier had been ill, but she did not know what had caused it. He had visited Bridge of Allan for the benefit of his health.
6   She remembered giving L'Angelier cocoa on one occasion at

some time in the past. He had barely sipped the drink. She had not given him anything to eat.

7   One of Madeleine's letters had made reference to a loaf of bread. She said that she had meant it as a joke. She thought that L'Angelier's illness might have been caused by a lack of food and this was why she had mentioned giving him bread.

8   She admitted having purchased quantities of arsenic three times. She claimed that she had used it for washing, diluted with water. It was a beauty tip she had been given by a young lady at her former school in Clapton. The young lady's name was Guibilei.

9   Her family did not know that she had been using arsenic in this way; she had kept it a secret. She had told the chemists that she wanted the arsenic to poison rats, because she did not want them to know that she was using it for cosmetic purposes.

10 William Minnoch had been visiting her home for several years. One month ago, he had proposed and she had accepted. The letter she had sent to L'Angelier on 20 March was to summon him so that she could tell him of her engagement to William Minnoch.

11 The cocoa that she used was kept on the mantelpiece in her room. She used hot water which the servants supplied to mix it.

12 She last used arsenic when she was preparing to go out to dinner at Mr Minnoch's house on 18 March.

13 She denied having given L'Angelier any arsenic.

Madeleine was tried in Edinburgh, in the June of that year. Her case had already attracted intense interest in her home town and the good citizens of Edinburgh were eager to hear further details. Accordingly, the trial was a sensation and the courtroom was packed to full capacity. Madeleine was charged with having given arsenic to L'Angelier on two occasions in February with the intent to kill him and with murdering him by administering arsenic to him again on an occasion in March.

There were too many of Madeleine's letters for all of them to be read out in court, but nearly sixty in total were to be used in evidence. They caused quite a stir and more than a few blushes in the courtroom. These were Victorian times; respectable people were prim, proper and prudish. To them, the content of some of Madeleine's letters was truly outrageous. But the letters that had been sent in reply by L'Angelier remained a mystery to the court. Madeleine had destroyed all his correspondence to her and the letters that were in the hands of the authorities were only draft copies that L'Angelier had kept himself. There was no proof that these were the same as the ones that had been sent to Madeleine. The pocketbook in which L'Angelier had begun to make entries shortly before the onset of his illness was never brought into court either. If it had been, it is hard to say whether its contents would have served the defence or the prosecution better.

Many witnesses were brought before the court, and gradually certain elements of L'Angelier's character were revealed. The prosecution sought to show that Madeleine was a wicked young woman, devoid of any sense of morality, the spider who drew L'Angelier into her web of sin and deceit and then killed him. The defence wanted to show that it was Madeleine who had been manipulated and that it was more likely that L'Angelier had taken his own life, possibly as a cruel and twisted act of revenge.

The evidence of forensic experts, who were brought to court by the prosecuting counsel, scored points for both sides in the trial. The prosecution was much reassured to hear how dangerous arsenic was when used as a cosmetic. It seemed less likely that Madeleine's story, that she used it for washing, was true. On the other hand, the quantity of arsenic that had been found in L'Angelier's stomach was very large indeed. Such a quantity would have been very difficult to disguise in a drink such as cocoa, for it would undoubtedly leave a gritty sediment in the bottom of the cup, which would arouse suspicion or at least distaste. The only way in which a large quantity of arsenic could be disguised in a drink of cocoa would be if the cocoa and the arsenic had been boiled up together with the water, for then it would be less likely to settle. Could Madeleine have worked out this clever method of concealing the poison? She said that she had made the cocoa with hot water brought to her by the servants, not that she had boiled it in the kitchen herself. Moreover, when such large quantities of arsenic had been found in a dead body, in the experts' previous experience, it was only when the poison had been taken deliberately rather than administered by another person.

Madeleine's letters, the basis for the prosecution's case against her, took a whole day to read. Her reputation as a 'nice' young lady was certainly ruined by their content, but was there anything in them that indicated that she was either vindictive or cruel enough to kill someone? Was there anything to prove that she intended to murder L'Angelier, or was even capable of such an act? The prosecution could certainly claim that she had a motive for murder – L'Angelier had become a real thorn in her side, after all – but there was nothing to prove beyond doubt that she had mixed the arsenic she had bought with cocoa and given it to him to drink. Moreover, there was no evidence to prove that she had seen L'Angelier on the night before he died, the night when the fatal dose was swallowed. Madeleine's sister Janet, with whom she shared a room, was unable to help the prosecution in any way. As far as she had been aware, Madeleine had gone to bed and slept right through the night in question. (Janet, of course, had been fast asleep and blissfully unaware of all the visits that L'Angelier had paid to Madeleine in the past.)

So was L'Angelier the sort of person who might consider committing suicide? Before he had come to Glasgow, L'Angelier had lived first in Edinburgh and then in Dundee. One of the witnesses for the defence was a man who had worked at the Rainbow Tavern in Edinburgh at the same time as L'Angelier was staying there for some months in 1851. The witness told the court that L'Angelier had been very low at that time – out of work and virtually penniless, and also suffering from disappointment in love. During that particular period he had talked of suicide on more than one occasion.

This witness was followed by another man, a trader, who had stayed at the Rainbow Tavern with L'Angelier and had talked to him on several occasions. This particular man had not taken to L'Angelier, finding him vain and boastful. On one occasion, however, he had met L'Angelier in town and had noticed that he was weeping. The source of his distress was apparently a young lady from Fife who had rejected him. L'Angelier had been in the habit of bragging about his success with the ladies and the trader felt that much of what he said was usually untrue, but on this occasion his distress had seemed genuine.

From Edinburgh, L'Angelier had moved to Dundee where he had found employment with a seed merchant. L'Angelier's employer, William Laird, told the court that he remembered L'Angelier as being very melancholy and apparently unwell in the first few weeks that he worked there. It turned out that he was upset about a girl with whom he had been in love. The girl had turned L'Angelier down in favour of another man, whom she was now going to marry. Once again, L'Angelier had talked of suicide, on more than one occasion, to more than one person at his place of work.

The defence then tried to show that there was a vindictive side to L'Angelier's nature. Another man who had known L'Angelier in Dundee told the court that L'Angelier had said to him that if he was jilted by a woman, he would take revenge upon her in some way. The way in which L'Angelier had behaved when Madeleine tried to put an end to the affair was also reprehensible. He had told a colleague at Huggins and Co. how upset he was when Madeleine had tried to end their affair. He also talked of his refusal to return Madeleine's letters to her and of his determination that she would never marry another man as long as he lived.

The defence called other witnesses who remembered L'Angelier talking about arsenic and showing a fair amount of knowledge about its effects. L'Angelier had told a man called David Hill, who worked with him at Laird's, that he used it regularly. Another man who became acquainted with L'Angelier recalled being told that L'Angelier had administered arsenic to horses while living in France to improve their powers of endurance on long journeys pulling a carriage. L'Angelier had freely admitted to using the drug himself for his complexion and to ease breathing problems. The same man had seen L'Angelier taking poppy seeds in generous quantities as well.

The defence had done their research quite thoroughly. L'Angelier had threatened suicide in the past and he had talked about revenge. In addition, he knew a good deal about arsenic and he had probably used it as well.

But it was Madeleine who had been buying arsenic in Glasgow, not L'Angelier. The defence was able to produce three witnesses to give evidence that perhaps L'Angelier had been doing a little shopping of his own. The three men were chemists who all owned shops in Glasgow, on the route that L'Angelier had probably taken on his way back from Bridge of Allan to his lodgings. All of them claimed that a man who looked like L'Angelier had come into their shops on Sunday 22 March and bought drugs. It was all rather vague, but it might have been enough to add a few more seeds of doubt to those that were already growing in the minds of the jury. Perhaps Madeleine Smith was not as guilty as she had at first appeared.

If the trial had taken place in England, then perhaps it would have been harder for the jury to reach a decision. In England they would have had to make a choice between only two verdicts – innocent or guilty. But the jury at the trial of Madeleine Smith had a third option, and they went for it quite rapidly. They took only thirty minutes or so to find that the murder charge against her was not proven. Madeleine Smith walked free from the court to the sound of cheers from many of the assembled crowd. Many others, however, still believed that she was guilty.

The Madeleine Smith case continues to rankle with people to this day. Seventy years after the death of the lady in question (she lived to a ripe old age, dying in 1928), people are still arguing about whether Madeleine was innocent or guilty. One side argues quite strenuously that she had the motive, the poison and the opportunity. She was also capable of deception: she had managed to carry on a clandestine relationship with L'Angelier for two years without the knowledge of her parents or, later, her fiancé, and she had also kept her forthcoming marriage to Minnoch a secret from L'Angelier. She was duplicitous, she was manipulative; she must have been guilty – she had to be. As recently as January 1999, an article published in a Scottish newspaper put forward another theory as to how Madeleine managed to get L'Angelier to take a large enough dose of arsenic to kill him. The spa water from Bridge of Allan contained arsenic, apparently, and if Madeleine had used a bottle of spa water to make the poisoned cocoa on that last fateful night, this, combined with a smaller dose of arsenic powder mixed in the drink, would have done the trick nicely. Perhaps it would have, but how can it be shown that Madeleine did give L'Angelier any spa water? Besides, L'Angelier could have drunk some spa water voluntarily; he had only just returned from Bridge of Allan himself.

Those who argue that Madeleine was innocent maintain that L'Angelier committed suicide, purely as an act of revenge against Madeleine, doing his utmost at the same time to put her in the frame for his murder. He made sure that several people knew of his illness before his death. He made a point of mentioning Madeleine and chocolate and poison together. He started his little journal before he died, the journal that noted his sickness on three occasions after seeing Madeleine, just in case the remarks he had made about his illness had gone unnoticed. Interestingly, the first mention of sickness in the journal was dated before Madeleine's first known purchase of arsenic. L'Angelier wrote that he was unwell on the night of 19/20 February. The first visit that Madeleine was known to have made to a chemist's to purchase arsenic was on 20 February, after that entry in L'Angelier's diary had been made. If she had put something in his drink on the night of 19 February, what was it and where had it come from?

L'Angelier was a vain little man who thought nothing of blackmailing the woman he professed to love. He had talked of suicide in the past when thwarted in love. He had also talked of revenge. He had pinned all his hopes on Madeleine, but in spite of all his efforts she had let him down. His only option was revenge and his best revenge would be suicide. Madeleine was innocent of his death.

There are, however, more than two possible answers to the riddle of L'Angelier's death. He might well have been poisoning himself, but he might not have intended to kill himself. He had spoken about suicide in the past, he had threatened to take his own life, but he had never, to anyone's knowledge, made a serious attempt at taking his own life. Why should he do so now? He had already resorted to one sort of blackmail to keep Madeleine. He had threatened to tell her father. If he took some arsenic, just enough arsenic to make him ill, he could use this against her as well, either as emotional blackmail (See what you made me do!) or, with the help of his journal and his pointed remarks to his friends, as a threat (I'll tell them you did this!) Poisoning oneself just enough to become ill requires a certain amount of precision and it would be very easy to make a tragic mistake. Perhaps this is what happened.

Another possibility is that both Madeleine and L'Angelier were responsible for his death. Perhaps, for every grain of arsenic that

Madeleine gave L'Angelier, he swallowed one of his own accord. Neither one need have known what the other was doing. If this was the case, then perhaps neither of them intended L'Angelier to die, but it is equally possible that both of them had had his death as their ultimate aim; remember, he had swallowed a very large quantity of the drug – more then enough to kill him.

The arguments may go on and on, but any conclusion that might be reached will be – has to be – only a matter of opinion.

Pierre Emile L'Angelier was buried in the family plot of his kindly employer, Mr Stevenson. Madeleine Smith left Glasgow and moved to London where she made herself known as Lena Smith ('Mimi' died with L'Angelier). She married a man called George Wardle, had two children and became a socialist. Wardle left her in 1889. Some years later, Madeleine moved to America and married again, becoming Lena Sheehy. She died in New York in April 1928. Her story, and all the speculation that surrounds it, is still very much alive today.

JESSIE McLACHLAN

On 7 July 1862, the body of a woman was found, partially dressed, in a bedroom in the basement of 17 Sandyford Place in Glasgow. The dead woman was Jess McPherson, a servant who worked in the house, which was owned by John Fleming, an accountant. Jess McPherson had been hacked to death with a cleaver.

The grisly find was made by John Fleming himself when he returned to the house, late in the afternoon, after a weekend in Dunoon with his family. John Fleming had left his father, James, in Sandyford Place, with Jess McPherson to look after him. But when he returned from Dunoon, his father told him that Jess was not at home and had been away all weekend. He had not seen her since Friday and he had assumed that she had gone off visiting. John Fleming was puzzled and went to Jess's room to investigate. He found it locked. Eventually, he managed to gain entry and found his servant's body sprawled on the floor beside the bed. She had been dead for some time.

The police were called. Their examination of the scene of the crime revealed that both the bedroom floor and the kitchen, which was next to the bedroom, had been cleaned up to some extent, but there were still signs that blood had been spilled. There was evidence that some parts in each room had been washed, but not very thoroughly. Jess's clothes chest had been disturbed and some of the clothes had smears of blood on them, as if someone had rummaged about in the contents of the box with bloodstained hands. Some of her good clothes were missing. Nothing else appeared to have been taken from the house apart from some silver-plated cutlery. There were bloodstains in various places: on some shirts in old Mr Fleming's wardrobe, in Jess's clothes chest, in the kitchen, at the back door, on the stairs up to the ground floor, and in Jess's bedroom. There were three clear, bloody footprints on Jess's bedroom floor, close to the side of the bed where the body was found.

It was inevitable that old Mr Fleming – James – should come under some suspicion. He had been in the same house as the body, probably for the whole weekend. Had he not been disturbed by Jess's unexplained absence? Had he not noticed the bloodstains around the basement? He was an old man, it was true – he was eighty-seven – but the blows to Jess's head and arms were not very deep. She had not died instantaneously from one almighty swipe. Whoever killed her had probably not been very strong.

James Fleming was arrested, questioned and imprisoned. At the same time, a pawnbroker, having read about the murder in the newspapers, came forward with some items of silver plate that had been pawned at his shop. They had been brought in by a woman who called herself Mary McDonald. The woman's name, and the address that she had given, were found to be false. The items were undoubtedly those that had been taken from 17 Sandyford Place, but who had the woman been?

James Fleming pointed the police in the direction of a woman called Jessie McLachlan. She fitted the description that the pawnbroker had given the police of the woman who had brought the silver plate to his shop. Both she and her husband were arrested, but her husband was soon released, having been away at sea when the killing took place.

Jessie was kept in custody and questioned at length. She used to work in the house in Sandyford Place before she was married. She had got along well with Jess McPherson and had remained friendly with her after she left the Flemings' employ – she admitted this freely. Jessie McLachlan also knew James Fleming. She had seen him at 17 Sandyford Place when she called to visit Jess McPherson and he had also been to her home.

Jessie McLachlan said in her statement that she had not seen Jess McPherson since 28 June. The meeting had taken place at her own house, not at Sandyford Place. McLachlan admitted that it had been she who had pawned the silver plate, but said that she had been asked to do so by James Fleming, who had brought it to her house at the Broomielaw on the evening of Friday 4 July.

Jessie McLachlan gave a long and involved statement to the police. At the same time, the police continued with investigations elsewhere that proved that almost everything she had told them was a lie.

The first lie:

Jessie McLachlan had said that she had been at home on the night of 4 July, with the exception of one brief outing late in the evening after ten o'clock. She had got back home at quarter past eleven.

The second lie:

Jessie McLachlan had said that she had let herself in to the building where she lived, using her own key.

This was not true. Mrs Campbell, who stayed in the same house, told police that Jessie had no key for the building. Furthermore, Jessie had been out all night, from Friday 4 July to Saturday 5 July at about nine in the morning. Jessie had left on Friday wearing a brown dress with flounces. When Mrs Campbell had let her in on Saturday morning, Jessie was wearing a new dress, which Mrs Campbell had not seen before.

The third lie:

Jessie had had a long and complicated explanation for the change of dress, but like her story about her whereabouts on the Friday night, it was all to be proved false. She said that the dress that she had been wearing on Friday night had been sent to be dyed on Saturday morning. But the police knew that the dress that went to the dyer's was not the brown dress that Jessie had been wearing on the Friday night, but another one – the dress that Mrs Campbell had seen her wearing when she arrived home on Saturday morning.

These three lies were to be the beginning of the undoing of Jessie McLachlan. She was now the prime suspect in the murder investigation.

More lies:

It turned out that Jessie did have some of Jess McPherson's clothes and had made some effort to conceal the fact by having them sent to Bridge Street Station in Glasgow. Her husband played a part in this revelation, telling the police where to find the clothes.

Jessie changed her story accordingly. Yes, she had been given the clothes by Jess McPherson to see to having some alterations done on them. Jessie McLachlan had been unable to see to the task at once and, when she heard of the death of Jess McPherson, the clothes were still in her possession. She had panicked and arranged for them to be sent away.

The brown dress that Jessie McLachlan had been wearing on the Friday night turned up as well. Jessie had sent another box to Hamilton. She said that the box had been meant to remain at Glasgow station, empty, until she filled it with clothes, for a visit to Hamilton. But the box had been sent on by mistake. She had intended going to Hamilton on the Saturday but had not gone until the Tuesday. She had not stayed as intended but had collected the box, still empty, from Hamilton and brought it home.

It all sounded rather too complicated. The police carried out a search at Hamilton and found torn pieces of the skirt of the brown dress and two ripped petticoats – all heavily bloodstained. Another piece of the brown dress was found in Jessie's house in the Broomielaw.

With every word that she said the case against Jessie McLachlan was getting stronger. To make matters worse, she was doing her best to implicate old James Fleming in the murder.

As she sat in prison one day, she had a visitor. The man who had come to see her asked her to step in some cow's blood and then to step on some planks of wood that he had brought with him. Jessie did so willingly and thus gave the case for the prosecution its trump card. Not long after this, old James Fleming was released from custody. The footprints that Jessie had made for her visitor in prison were almost an exact match of the footprints that were found in Jess McPherson's bedroom. The prosecution could place Jessie McLachlan in the basement of 17 Sandyford Place around the time of the killing. It was therefore unlikely, in their opinion, that James Fleming had anything to do with the sordid affair.

Jessie had dug herself deep into trouble.

The trial took place in the High Court in Glasgow, starting on 17 September. After the story of the discovery of Jess McPherson's body had been told, old James Fleming took his place in the witness box. He had last seen Jess McPherson alive on Friday night, he said. He had spent some time in the kitchen with her before he went up to bed at about nine-thirty.

During the night, he had been woken by the sound of a squeal, which had been repeated two or three times. He had looked at his watch and seen that it was four o'clock in the morning. As it was summer time, it was already light outside.

This part of James Fleming's story concurs with the stories of witnesses in the street who had been alerted to something going on at 17 Sandyford Place by the sounds of moaning or at least similar noises. A light had also been noticed burning in the house.

James Fleming said that he had eventually got up and dressed at about nine o'clock. Jess usually brought him porridge in the morning, and when she did not appear he went to her room and knocked on the door, but there had been no answer.

James Fleming said he got up at nine o'clock, but the milk boy said that the old man had answered the door to him that Saturday morning, fully dressed, not long after seven thirty.

Jessie's defence tried to make something of this discrepancy but did not get very far.

Why had Fleming answered the door to the milk boy rather than waiting for Jess McPherson to answer? This would be the normal course of events, surely!

Jess wasn't there. Jess was dead.

Did James Fleming know that Jess was dead?

No.

Did James Fleming know the accused?

Yes, but he had not seen her for a year. No, he had not asked her to pawn the silver plate.

Previously, James Fleming had denied any acquaintance with Jessie McLachlan, in spite of her having worked in the house in Sandyford Place a while before.

James Fleming's story was beginning to fall to pieces, but for some reason the judge, Lord Deas, would let Jessie McLachlan's defence counsel go no further. James Fleming was allowed to stand down from the witness box.

The defence continued with its efforts to discredit Fleming after he left the witness box. Witnesses were brought forward to tell how Jess McPherson was pestered continuously by the amorous advances of the old man. Fleming had also been brought before the kirk session in time gone by to answer for similar behaviour.

But it was not enough. Jessie McLachlan was poor. She might well be tempted to help herself to a bit of silver plate. James Fleming was well off. Why would he need to pawn anything?

Jessie McLachlan had lied repeatedly in statements she had

made. She had made efforts to conceal a bloodstained dress. She had also tried to hide the fact that she had been in possession of some of Jess McPherson's clothes. It was plain that she was the one who had killed Jess McPherson and that her motive was personal gain.

Things looked bleak when the jury went out to consider its verdict. It took them minutes only to reach their decision. Guilty.

Before sentence was passed, Jessie McLachlan's last statement was read to the court. The story had changed again, but it is probably the closest she had ever come to telling the truth about what happened to Jess McPherson. The statement was long and detailed, but the essence of it was as follows:

Jessie had gone to see Jess McPherson on the night of Friday 4 July, taking some rum with her. She had sat with Jess and James Fleming in the kitchen. Both had already been drinking. After some time, Jessie had gone out to get more drink. When she got back, she found Jess on the floor, cut and bleeding from the head. As she attended to her friend, she learned that Jess had been angry with Fleming for some time because of his lewd behaviour towards her. Things had come to a head some weeks before and the argument had started up again on this particular night when Jessie McLachlan had gone out to buy more drink. Fleming had lost his temper and attacked Jess McPherson.

It seemed that the old man was now repentant, and he helped Jessie McLachlan clean McPherson's wounds and settle her in bed.

During the night Jess had taken a turn for the worse. McLachlan's dress was in a poor state, smeared with blood and wet after her efforts to clean her friend's wounds, so she had put on one of Jess McPherson's dresses. She had then told the old man that she was going out to get a doctor. She had gone up to the front door but, finding it locked, she had come back down. She found Jess was worse. The old man, however, had urged her not to go for help. He was frightened of the consequences of his actions. He did not want anyone to find out, either from Jess or from Jessie, what he had done.

Jessie McLachlan had been persuaded not to leave but had gone upstairs again to look out of the window to see if there was any sign of life in the neighbouring houses. When she came back down again, she found the old man striking the fatal blows to Jess McPherson with the meat cleaver.

Fleming had persuaded McLachlan, by telling her that she was in danger of being implicated in the murder if she told anyone, to help him to clean up the scene of the crime and take Jess's body back into her bedroom. In order to make it look as if there had been a robbery, Fleming had given McLachlan the silver-plate cutlery to pawn under an assumed name. He had also told her to send some of Jess's clothes away somewhere by train and advised her to send her own bloodstained clothes away also, to be disposed of in some far-off place.

The statement did not prevent the judge from passing the death sentence on Jessie McLachlan. But by now, followers of the trial were divided into two camps: one that believed in her guilt, another that thought that Fleming was the guilty party. There was a public outcry at the sentence, and eventually, after an inquiry, Jessie McLachlan was given a reprieve and sentenced to life imprisonment instead.

The fuss took a long time to die down. Yet another statement made by Jessie McLachlan before she went for trial was published after the trial. In this statement she implicated herself in Jess McPherson's death, but it had been more or less dismissed as hysterical rambling. The papers were full of theories about the case. Much was made of Fleming's lascivious nature.

But none of the fuss, or speculation, or revelations, was enough to release Jessie from her prison sentence. She served a full fifteen years – the normal length of a life sentence in those days.

Jessie McLachlan was eventually released from prison in 1877.

Old Fleming was never brought to answer any charges relating to the case, but public opinion turned against him and his life was made very difficult for quite some time after the trial.

The real truth is still not known. Jessie McLachlan was almost certainly present when her friend was killed – she had admitted that much herself – but what part did she play in the affair? Fleming undoubtedly had a great deal more to do with it than he would ever admit. He probably did kill Jess McPherson. He had every reason to want her to be silenced. But the problem was that James Fleming was cleverer than Jessie. He knew when to keep his mouth shut. Had Jessie McLachlan told the whole truth in the first instance, she might have escaped prison altogether. Her final statement before sentencing was probably true for the most part. Careful analysis many years later of Jessie's statement and of the statements given by witnesses at the time of the murder indicated that they concurred and that Jessie was most likely innocent. But compelled as she was to tell a string of fabrications, she very nearly dug her own grave.

DR PRITCHARD

Edward William Pritchard was a liar and throughout his adult life he told lie after lie to worm his way into respectable society, to convince those whom he encountered that he was a better, brighter, more important man than he really was, to influence those whom he wished to use for his own purposes. During his trial, facts emerged about this extraordinary man that convinced those who read about the case that not only did he lie to serve his own immediate ends, but he also lied for the fun of it. He enjoyed lying.

On 28 July 1865, Dr Pritchard was hanged for murder. Two cases of murder had been proven, another was suspected. The trial had been a sensation, and the execution, the last public hanging in Scotland, was reported in great detail in the papers. Amongst those who wrote about the trial was William Roughead, an Edinburgh lawyer and a celebrated criminologist. When he wrote about the case, he was to conclude that the real motive behind all Dr Pritchard's terrible crimes was enjoyment. Not only did Dr Pritchard lie because he enjoyed it; he killed people, too, just for pleasure.

Edward William Pritchard was born in 1825 in Southsea. He came from a naval background. His father, his uncles and his brothers all had distinguished careers in the navy, and Edward himself began his working life when he was fifteen, apprenticed to naval surgeons.

In 1846 Pritchard was admitted to the College of Surgeons. He claimed to have attended King's College, London, but the college denied anyone of that name having attended there. Although Pritchard was obviously clever and knowledgeable enough to convince the College of Surgeons of his abilities, his true credentials as a doctor have to be in doubt.

From 1846 to 1850 Pritchard served on various ships in the Royal Navy and travelled widely. In 1850 he met and married a young Edinburgh woman. Her name was Mary Jane Taylor and she was the daughter of a wealthy merchant, Michael Taylor. It was the generosity of his new wife's parents that helped to buy Pritchard out of the Navy in 1851 and set him up in practice in Humanby, Yorkshire. The couple stayed there for nine years, in the course of which time five children were born.

During the family's time in Humanby, Pritchard's reputation as a liar and a womaniser was better established in the minds of many of the people in the surrounding area than his reputation as a doctor. He enjoyed prominence and wormed his way into membership of the Freemasons. He practised his profession in Humanby and Filey and made the most of the position in society that his profession afforded him, becoming intimately acquainted with several of his female patients. He lived beyond his means, by all accounts, and accumulated considerable debts, but he was still able to buy himself further qualifications to improve his professional image. Thus he purchased his diploma as a doctor of medicine from the University of Erlangen and later as a Licentiate of the Society of Apothecaries of London. These bogus qualifications certainly sounded good and they probably looked good as well, gilded certificates framed and hanging on the walls of his consulting room.

In 1860, having sold his practice in Yorkshire, Pritchard arrived in Glasgow and took up residence in Berkeley Street. He continued his involvement with the Freemasons and within two years was elected master of Lodge St Mark. He also became a member of the Glasgow Royal Arch Chapter and of the Grand Lodge of the Royal Order in Edinburgh. However, he was less successful in his attempts to impress the medical profession in Glasgow and the eminent surgeons and physicians of the city were very suspicious of his credentials. Undaunted, Pritchard continued to tell extravagant lies about the life he had led, the experiences he had had and the knowledge he had acquired. He frequently gave lectures on the places he claimed to have visited and was quite unperturbed when he was accused of making things up. What did it matter if some people did not believe him? There were plenty of people who did, who could give that extra sheen to his well-polished sense of his own importance. He was quite an expert in self-promotion; his visiting card, complete with his picture in full Masonic regalia, was a testament to the vanity of the man. His womanising continued much as before.

In 1863 there was a fire at Dr Pritchard's house in Berkeley Street. Elizabeth McGirn, a servant, lost her life in the blaze. The police were suspicious about the incident and most of their suspicions centred on the doctor. However, after initial investigations, they took the matter no further. There is little doubt in the minds of those who are familiar with the story of Dr Pritchard and his subsequent crimes that he was responsible for the death of Elizabeth McGirn. If the investigating authorities had been able to call upon the services of forensic scientists and the knowledge that they have nowadays, perhaps Pritchard would have been prevented from committing his next two murders.

The fire had broken out at night. Dr Pritchard claimed he was roused from sleep by his sons, who had been woken by the smoke. He had gone up to the attic floor, where the smoke was coming from, to investigate but had been prevented from going into Elizabeth's room by the denseness of the smoke.

A policeman in the area had also noticed the smoke and rung the front door bell. When Dr Pritchard answered, he was fully dressed (in spite of his claims that he had just been woken from sleep). The fire brigade was called, but the firemen were too late to save Elizabeth McGirn. Her body was found, horribly burnt, lying on her bed.

It was strange that the girl had not been woken by the smoke. The normal reaction would be for her to have choked and roused. She might not have been able to escape, but she ought to have been sufficiently aware of what was going on to try. Why had this not happened? Was she sedated or already dead when the fire broke out? No one could tell in those days.

Dr Pritchard aroused further suspicion when he made considerable claims to his insurance company for a quantity of jewellery that he said had been destroyed in the fire. No sign of anything of that nature was found in the aftermath of the blaze. Dr Pritchard eventually agreed to settle for a fraction of the amount that he had claimed.

The good doctor carried on regardless. The family moved from Berkeley Street to Royal Crescent, then to 131 Sauchiehall Street, kindly purchased for them by Mary Jane's mother. Although Pritchard had been strongly suspected of having adulterous relations with Elizabeth McGirn, one of the reasons why he was questioned so closely after her death, he did not hesitate to avail himself of the pleasures of her successor, Mary McLeod. His relationship with Mary was anything but discreet, and his wife, Mary Jane, found out about it. Mary McLeod became pregnant and had to have an abortion, carried out by Pritchard, but their relationship continued and McLeod was kept interested by promises of marriage should Mrs Pritchard chance to die before her.

Mrs Pritchard started to become ill in the autumn of 1864. The problem appeared to be some sort of gastric upset. She went to stay with her parents in Edinburgh, and the change seemed to do her good for she felt much better. She went back home in time for the festive season, only to take another turn for the worse. She was really very unwell and had to spend long periods in bed. Dr Pritchard, playing the part of the solicitous husband to the full, showed great concern. Quite often he would take meals and drinks up to her himself.

By February Mary Jane Pritchard was becoming seriously ill. She had periods of retching and vomiting, stomach pains and cramp in her hands. Dr Pritchard invited Mary Jane's cousin, Dr James Cowan, from Edinburgh, to visit. Dr Cowan was not too concerned about Mary Jane's condition but recommended that Mrs Taylor be invited to come and stay as a comfort to her daughter.

Mary Jane grew worse. She was in great distress. Another doctor was called, Dr Gairdner, Professor of Medicine at Glasgow University. Dr Pritchard told his colleague that Mary Jane had a stomach upset and that he had given her chloroform and champagne on the instructions of Dr Cowan.

Dr Gairdner found Mary Jane in a state of hysteria. In some ways, she had the appearance of a drunkard, but her hands were seized by some sort of spasm. Dr Gairdner visited twice, advising Dr Pritchard against the use of chloroform and prescribing a diet of bread and milk for the patient. Dr Gairdner then wrote to Dr Taylor, Mary Jane's brother, expressing his concern about the treatment that Dr Pritchard had been giving her. Dr Taylor tried to have his sister sent down to stay with him in Penrith for treatment and recuperation, but Dr Pritchard insisted that his wife was too ill to make the journey.

Dr Gairdner was right to be concerned about Mary Jane's treatment. Dr Pritchard may have been truthful in admitting to giving his wife chloroform and champagne, but he had omitted to tell his colleague of the purchases he had made at the chemist's in November, when Mary Jane's illness began, and then again in February the next year. These purchases were of tincture of aconite and tartarised antimony. Both are poisons and, in the amounts in which Dr Pritchard had purchased them, deadly. Had Dr Gairdner or Dr Cowan been aware of these purchases they might have realised what lay behind Mary Jane Pritchard's strange malaise.

Mrs Taylor arrived to attend to her daughter, and over the course of the next few days there was some improvement. It was probably more difficult for Pritchard to 'administer' to his sickly wife while he was under the eagle eye of his mother-in-law.

One day the cook made some tapioca pudding for the patient. The packet, newly bought, was left by the message boy outside Dr Pritchard's consulting room for a while before the cook collected it to make the pudding. Dr Pritchard had his chance to continue with his wife's 'treatment'.

The pudding was taken up to Mary Jane's room, but she felt too unwell to eat it. Her mother ate the tapioca instead – and was violently ill as a consequence.

On 24 February Mrs Taylor fell suddenly ill. Dr Pritchard summoned another doctor, Dr James Paterson. Telling Dr Paterson that Mrs Taylor and Mrs Pritchard had both become sick after drinking beer with their evening meal, Dr Pritchard announced that Mrs Taylor was suffering from apoplexy.

Dr Paterson found both women in Mary Jane Pritchard's bed. Mrs Taylor appeared to be drugged. Her daughter was in a state of extreme weakness and distress.

Dr Paterson saw that Mrs Taylor was dying and diagnosed an overdose of some narcotic. Dr Pritchard informed Dr Paterson that yes, indeed, Mrs Taylor had been in the habit of taking increasing amounts of Battley's Sedative Solution. Her taste for it must have overwhelmed her tolerance.

Dr Paterson had his own suspicions but could not prove them.

Mary Jane's illness was clearly different. Dr Paterson suspected that she was suffering from antimony poisoning – her symptoms fitted the bill – but of course, he could prove nothing.

Mrs Taylor died the next day. When the registrar asked Dr Paterson to fill in a form giving the cause of Mrs Taylor's death, he promptly wrote back refusing to do so. Dr Pritchard obligingly completed the death certificate himself, giving cause of death as paralysis followed by apoplexy.

Dr Paterson attended Mary Jane Pritchard again while her

husband attended Mrs Taylor's funeral, but some days later Dr Pritchard called to say that he would no longer be requiring his services. His wife was getting better. The truth was that Dr Paterson knew a little too much for Dr Pritchard's comfort.

Needless to say, Mrs Pritchard was not getting better at all. Dr Pritchard had bought some more tincture of aconite, and as a consequence Mary Jane grew sicker. Sometimes other members of the household suffered symptoms that were very similar. Mary McLeod, still retained in the household as servant and concubine of Dr Pritchard, became ill when she tasted a piece of cheese intended for Mary Jane's consumption. The cook, Mary Patterson, suffered similarly.

Gradually Mrs Pritchard's condition grew worse. The periods of retching and vomiting continued, and by mid-March, she had become quite deranged. On 17 March, Dr Paterson was summoned again and he prescribed some medication for the patient to sedate her. Dr Pritchard took details of the prescription but never had it filled. In the early hours of the following morning, his wife was dead.

Dr Pritchard went to great lengths to play the grieving husband. He filled in his wife's death certificate himself, giving gastric fever as cause of death, but others were not convinced.

On 20 March an anonymous letter arrived at the office of the Procurator Fiscal in Glasgow. The letter is thought to have been written by Dr Paterson. It stated that Dr Pritchard's mother-in-law had died three weeks before and that now his wife had died suddenly and unexpectedly. Both deaths had taken place under suspicious circumstances and action should be taken to 'see justice done'.

The letter had the desired effect, and police inquiries were soon under way.

Meanwhile, Dr Pritchard was attending to his wife's funeral arrangements. Mary Jane's body was taken to her parents' home in Edinburgh. There the coffin was opened at Dr Pritchard's insistence to allow viewing of the body. In an astonishing display of hypocrisy, the doctor leant over his wife's body and kissed her tenderly on her lips.

On his return to Glasgow Dr Pritchard was arrested. The 'good' doctor protested his innocence very strenuously, and his performance during the previous few months must have been quite convincing, for there were still many people who believed him. He had quite a few visitors in prison. But Mrs Taylor's body was exhumed and Mary Jane's body was examined and both were found to contain large quantities of antimony. The case against him was getting stronger. For a short while, Mary McLeod fell under suspicion as well, but she was released quite shortly after her arrest.

On 3 July 1865 the case went to trial in Edinburgh. Dr Pritchard made quite a striking figure in court, for he was quite a handsome man and the appearance of calm and innocence that he affected was remarkably convincing. Five days later, when the trial was over, he was still tranquil in demeanour, but his confidence was undeniably shaken.

Mary McLeod had been asked to give evidence, and the longstanding affair between her and Dr Pritchard came to light. Not only that, but the court learned of the abortion Mary McLeod had had, with the assistance of Dr Pritchard. There was no proof that Dr Pritchard himself had actually administered the poison to his wife and mother-in-law, but there was proof that he had bought lethal quantities of poison on at least four occasions. Dr Pritchard's defence team tried to lay some of the blame at Mary McLeod's feet, but their efforts were pointless. Dr Paterson was brought before the court as a witness, and he told of his early suspicions that both Mrs Taylor and Mrs Pritchard were being poisoned. He had written to the registrar refusing to sign Mrs Taylor's death certificate in the hope that Dr Pritchard would take fright and stop poisoning his wife. Professional etiquette had prevented him from alerting the authorities to what he thought was going on.

Dr Paterson was condemned for his reticence. His attention to 'professional etiquette' had prevented him from saving Mary Jane, but at least his evidence helped to bring Dr Pritchard to justice at last.

The jury did not take long to reach their verdict. Dr Pritchard was guilty of double murder. The accused stayed quiet and calm right to the end. He showed little emotion during the trial, with the exception of one occasion when the evidence of one of his children moved him to tears. Were the tears genuine? We cannot tell. The man was a convincing actor, after all.

When sentence was pronounced, he bowed to acknowledge what had been said. The sentence was death, to take place in Glasgow. Dr Pritchard was led out of court.

In the three weeks that were left to him until his death, Dr Pritchard continued to lie as he had always done. He put on a great display of religious piety, spending a great deal of his time with various visiting ministers. Whether he thought that his behaviour was likely to bring about a miraculous change in his fate or whether he was simply compelled to carry on with his perpetual pretending we shall never know. A third explanation for Dr Pritchard's increasing preoccupation with God and the scriptures, that he might feel genuine remorse for his actions and be seeking God's forgiveness, is the most unlikely.

He did, by very roundabout means, eventually confess to his crimes. First of all he admitted killing his wife, saying that he had given her an overdose of chloroform. He implied that Mary McLeod was an accessory to the fact. In the second version of events that he gave, he admitted that he had been involved in an adulterous affair with Mary McLeod and had caused her to have a miscarriage. He declared that his wife had been aware of the affair. He said that although Mrs Taylor had also found out about Mary McLeod, she had not died by his hand but by her own, from an overdose of Battley's Sedative Solution. He had succumbed to temptation whilst under the influence of drink and given his wife a fatal dose of chloroform. Mary McLeod had been present; indeed, it was his involvement with her that had caused 'some species of madness' compelling him to kill Mrs Pritchard.

Finally, Dr Pritchard admitted that he had acted alone and that he had killed both Mrs Taylor and his wife. However, rather than admitting to killing his wife slowly and carefully, as he did, over a period of more than three months, he still blamed his actions on a combination of madness and drink.

On 28 July 1865, Edward William Pritchard was hanged in Glasgow in front of a crowd of almost 100,000 people.

EUGENE MARIE CHANTRELLE

Eugene Marie Chantrelle was a very intelligent man, of that there can be no doubt. He was born in Nantes in France in 1834, into the family of a wealthy shipping magnate. The young Eugene did very well academically and was eventually enrolled in medical school, ready for what promised to be a successful and profitable career as a doctor. However, before he had the chance to complete his studies, his father's business foundered as a direct result of the revolution in 1848 and the family faced considerable financial difficulties. Eugene found himself without the necessary funding to complete his course and had to give it up. Was this where his anger came from, or was there something else in his character or background that provoked him into acting in the way he did in the years to come? No one can tell.

Chantrelle's career path took a few different turns in the years after that. He continued with some classes but only sporadically and without conclusion. He became a sympathiser for the Republican party and took part in the coup d'état in 1851. He was wounded in the affray, receiving a sabre blow to the arm. Shortly afterwards, probably motivated by a desire for self-preservation, he sailed for America.

Little is known of Chantrelle's activities whilst he was in America. He finally returned to Europe in the 1860s, spending some time in England before choosing, in 1866, to settle in Edinburgh for a while. He was intelligent, articulate and charming, and soon he was a popular figure in Edinburgh's polite society. The darker side of his nature was well concealed from public view. To the outside world he was highly respectable and thoroughly likeable.

It was without difficulty that Chantrelle secured himself a position at a private school in Edinburgh, Newington Academy. He was fluent in English, Latin and German and his native tongue was of course French. His skills would make him a useful asset as a language tutor.

One of his pupils at the academy was a girl called Elizabeth Cullen Dyer. She was fifteen but very mature physically and quite knowing in the ways of the world. She and Chantrelle were mutually attracted and embarked upon an affair within a short time. Inevitably, Elizabeth became pregnant. The couple were married in 1868, two months before the child, the first of three, was born. There is little doubt that Chantrelle married Elizabeth not from love but because it was more in his interest to stay in Edinburgh and with her than it was to leave and have to start anew elsewhere. Elizabeth may have hoped for happiness with her lover, but it is more than likely that Chantrelle saw the relationship as a convenient sexual dalliance that had gone awry rather than as a marriage of true minds or hearts. He was thirty-four, ruthless and ambitious. She was but seventeen years old when they married and reduced by the pregnancy to helplessness and utter dependency upon him. The omens were not good.

The marriage was not a happy one. Chantrelle treated his young wife very badly. He got into the habit of drinking heavily and was often violent towards Elizabeth. His respectable reputation around Edinburgh became tarnished as he continued to drink and took to visiting brothels to satisfy his carnal urges. Fuelled by drink, he was known to have moments of uncontrollable rage both in the home and in public. Most damning of all, he threatened to kill Elizabeth on more than one occasion. Elizabeth, for her part, was unable to find any real source of help to get her out of her miserable predicament.

Eugene Chantrelle's profligate lifestyle could not be maintained on his schoolmaster's salary. Nine years on, the family was deep in debt. The Frenchman might have been a drunk, but his mind was clear enough to work out the potential profit he could make from Elizabeth's demise. After making some inquiries, he took out an insurance policy on his wife's life. In the event of her death, he would receive the princely sum of £1000, which was a substantial amount of money in those days. It was December 1877. Elizabeth was not a fool. She could see the way in which her husband's mind was working and realised perfectly well that her life was in danger. She told her parents of her fears, but they dismissed them as pure fancy.

Elizabeth's fears were tragically confirmed on New Year's Day, barely a week after her husband had taken out the assurance policy. On Hogmanay, the family spent some time together and Eugene ushered in the New Year in the company of his wife with drinks and confections. An uneasy peace seemed to have settled over the turbulent household in George Street. However, the next day Elizabeth was complaining of feeling unwell. Eugene was remarkably solicitous during the course of the day, but Elizabeth continued to complain that she felt unwell. She vomited in the afternoon and was too nauseous to join the family at dinner. She went to bed, still feeling very low, but managed to eat some fruit. Her husband retired later, going to sleep in another room with the children.

It was the household maid who first found Elizabeth the next morning in a state of semi-consciousness. The maid alerted Chantrelle, who came at once and told her to watch out for the children while he attended to his wife. The maid came back into the room shortly afterwards and found Chantrelle opening the window, complaining of a strong smell of gas. The maid had not noticed any such smell when she had found her mistress but did not question her master. She turned off the gas supply and went at his bidding to find a doctor.

The doctor took some time to come. By the time he reached the Chantrelles' flat, there was a strong smell of gas in Elizabeth's room. Elizabeth's condition was getting worse and another doctor was summoned swiftly. Attempts to revive her were failing, and shortly afterwards she was removed to the Royal Infirmary. There, late in the afternoon, she died.

The two doctors who had visited Elizabeth at home had not questioned Chantrelle's declarations that his wife had died from gas poisoning, but the doctor in the infirmary who examined her found evidence to the contrary. Her symptoms pointed to narcotic poisoning rather than gas inhalation. The next day a post-mortem examination was carried out and the doctors were still baffled.

Meanwhile, gas men had been called to the flat in George Street to find the leak. A gas pipe in Elizabeth's room had been broken. It was no ordinary leak. It looked as if the pipe had been bent backwards and forwards until it cracked.

Chantrelle was still officially in the clear, no matter how suspicious people were. Elizabeth had not died from gas poisoning, so the broken pipe proved nothing. Nor had any other cause of death been established beyond doubt. Chantrelle was free to go ahead with his wife's funeral, playing the part of the desolate grieving spouse with gusto. No doubt, as he stood at her graveside, he looked forward to the day when the cheque would arrive from the insurance company.

What Chantrelle did not know was that the investigations into Elizabeth's death had not stopped after the post-mortem. She had vomited during the course of the night before she died and she had vomit on her night-clothes and in her hair. Prudently, the doctor in charge of her case had taken samples for analysis. The samples, along with samples of fluid taken from her stomach after death, showed that Elizabeth had swallowed a substantial amount of extract of opium. Bits of fruit in her vomit were also found to contain the poison.

Chantrelle was arrested, and both his flat and his study at school were searched. Chemists' records were checked. A substantial amount of poisons were found in a cache in Chantrelle's study – for what purpose? Following checking with the records held by chemists in the area, it was discovered that Chantrelle had purchased lethal amounts of opium extract from one chemist. The opium was nowhere to be found amongst the horde of drugs that the police found in Chantrelle's study, and Chantrelle could neither produce it nor offer any reasonable explanation for its disappearance.

The trial of Eugene Marie Chantrelle took pace in May 1878. Chantrelle's defence worked hard to try to prove that their client was innocent of murder, but in vain. Chantrelle himself appeared as a pathetic figure in the dock. Deprived of the alcohol upon which he had so heavily relied in recent years, he seemed ill, twitchy and angry – almost deranged. His claims that his wife had committed suicide were dismissed. He was found guilty and sentenced to death.

After sentencing, Chantrelle was given the chance to address the court, but far from showing remorse for what he had done, he continued to deny most strenuously that he had had anything to do with his wife's death. This attitude prevailed when an appeal was mounted against his sentence.

The appeal failed. Chantrelle was executed on 31 May 1878 at eight o'clock in the morning, in Calton Prison in Edinburgh. Those who gathered on the hill, hoping to see him as he walked the short distance to the gallows from his cell, were disappointed. The area was screened off and the execution was kept private.

Right up to the moment of his own death, Chantrelle maintained that he was innocent and showed no sign of repentance.

JESSIE KING

The twentieth century has seen an enormous change in attitudes towards love, marriage and children in our society. Some people will bemoan the fact that the institution of marriage does not seem to be taken as seriously as it once was. What has happened to family life? What is the future for it when unmarried couples can live together quite freely, one in three marriages end in divorce and many people, particularly women, bring up their children alone?

Perhaps things have changed a little too much for some people's comfort, but it cannot be denied that many of these changes are for the better. One hundred years ago, a child born out of wedlock was destined for a fairly miserable life. An unmarried mother's position in society was hopeless. 'Victorian values' were all very well, but they did not prevent the consummation of illicit passions, the seduction of a servant girl by her master, the adulterous affair or the careless coupling fuelled by alcohol. Victorian values stepped in when the damage had been done, when the child had been conceived. Condemnation fell upon both mother and innocent child. The man, on the other hand, could safely disappear into the mist, free to do the same again, to another woman, in another place, at another time.

Unplanned and unwanted pregnancies spelled disaster. Many women died as the result of botched attempts at aborting the child that they carried. Some concealed the pregnancy until full term and then quietly disposed of the baby. Other babies were abandoned, left to their fate in dark passageways and corners, where, if they were fortunate, they might be discovered by some kind soul who might take care of them or else put them into the 'care' of the authorities.

To those who chose to avail themselves of her services, Jessie King must have appeared as a godsend.

Jessie lived with her partner, Michael Pearson. In 1887, the couple had lodgings in Dalkeith Road in Edinburgh and scraped together enough cash to keep them in food and, more importantly, drink from Pearson's casual labouring jobs. The couple had no children of their own – they had not been together long enough, as it transpired – but in the late summer of 1887, they answered an advert for foster parents for the child of Elizabeth Campbell. Elizabeth was dead – she had died in childbirth – and neither her family nor the baby's father wanted the responsibility of raising her illegitimate child. They did not hesitate when Jessie and Pearson, calling themselves Stewart, came to call. They handed over the child to these eager strangers, along with a generous fee. Jessie and Pearson took the baby home to Dalkeith Road. They looked after it for a while, and by all accounts the baby was thriving. Then, as unexpectedly as the child had arrived, it had gone. Jessie told those who asked her that the baby had been given a home by an aunt.

Some months later Jessie answered another advert. The advert was for foster parents to look after Alexander, the child of Catherine Gunn, a girl in domestic service. This time Jessie called herself Mrs Macpherson when she made her application. The child was handed over, once again with a generous fee, and Jessie took him home with her to the lodgings in Canonmills where she and Pearson were now staying. Once again it seemed as if Jessie was taking reasonable care of her charge. The baby seemed quite healthy, and Jessie made sure that he was looked after by another woman when she was out. Then, once again, the child suddenly vanished. If Jessie's explanation as to where the child had gone was unsettlingly vague, her tone was certainly reassuring. The little boy was fine, she said. Shortly afterwards, possibly to avoid further awkward questions from neighbours or from the baby's natural relatives, Jessie and Pearson moved out and found a place to live in Stockbridge.

Their new home was in Cheyne Street, and their landlords were the Banks family. It was not long before the Banks family began to feel uneasy about 'Mr and Mrs McPherson', their new lodgers.

In September 1888 Jessie brought a baby home to Cheyne Street. It was a little girl this time. She was the bastard child of a girl called Violet Tomlinson. The little girl did not stay long at her new home, however. She was gone again, almost as soon as she had arrived. Jessie was inconsistent in the stories that she told to Mr and Mrs Banks and their daughter, both about who the child was and where she had disappeared to.

One month later some children playing on some grass close to the house in Cheyne Street made a grisly discovery. Coming upon a dirty parcel wrapped up in oilskin, they unwrapped it and found the body of a dead baby. Examination of the body by the police revealed that the child had been strangled.

The Banks family remembered the baby that their lodgers had brought home so briefly and put two and two together. They told the police of their suspicions and a visit was paid to Jessie. Jessie admitted that she had been looking after a baby for a short while but insisted the child was now in the care of her sister. Then the police began a search, and Jessie broke down. She showed the officers to the coal cupboard, which was locked. When the policemen opened the door and looked inside, they were shocked to find another baby's body.

The baby that had been found outside was a boy. This one was a girl and was, in fact, the baby that the Banks had seen Jessie with at Cheyne Street. The baby boy had been dead for much longer – he was Alexander Gunn.

Jessie was arrested and taken into custody where, under questioning, she admitted killing both babies. She claimed that although she was very fond of little Alexander, caring for him had become so much of a burden that she had finally strangled him in a drunken fit of depression. She had wrapped the body up and hidden it, and not knowing what else to do had brought it to Cheyne Street, like a piece of luggage, when they moved. The child of Violet Tomlinson had died completely by accident. Jessie had fed her whisky to stop her crying and had overdone it. She had now been faced with having two dead babies on her hands. She put the body of the Tomlinson baby in the coal cupboard where she had been concealing Alexander Gunn, and took his body out. Did she really think it was safe enough to leave the macabre parcel outside on the green or was her decision to leave it there borne of sheer panic? We will never know.

In time it was discovered that Jessie had been given care of another child: the Campbell baby, the first to disappear. A third murder charge was added to the first two.

Jessie would be found guilty of murder, of that there was no doubt. But what had made her kill these poor babies? Was it simply a matter of economics – the money for their care had run out, so they had to go? Or was she genuinely fond of the children but simply too inadequate to cope with the demands that caring for them placed upon her? It was a perplexing question. If she had taken the children purely for profit, then why had she kept them for any time at all? Alexander Gunn had certainly been given a reasonable amount of care; there were witnesses to testify to that. Elizabeth Campbell's baby had seemed to be doing quite well in Jessie's home until she disappeared. (The murder charge against Jessie for the Campbell baby had to be dropped eventually; Jessie denied having killed the baby and there was no body to prove her guilt.)

If Jessie had genuinely tried to care for Alexander Gunn but had failed so miserably, why did she apply to adopt another baby – the Tomlinson baby – only a few months later?

Jessie made a rather pathetic figure standing in the dock listening to the evidence against her. As those in the courtroom listened to the details of the case, they cannot just have been wondering about Jessie's motives. They must also have wondered what on earth could persuade anyone to give a child to a person like that. There is no doubt about it: for some people in those days, life was cheap.

Pearson was not charged with murder along with Jessie. He might or might not have had something to do with the deaths of the children – he had certainly played his part in procuring them – but it was Jessie who was held entirely responsible for the two murder charges. The trial did not last long. She was sentenced to hang on 11 March; calls for a reprieve were unsuccessful. Jessie King spent her last days on earth in abject despair, trying to make her peace with God. She was executed on 11 March 1889 in Calton Prison. She was the second last woman to be hanged for murder in Scotland.

DEATH ON GOATFELL

Arran is a beautiful island in the Firth of Clyde. It has always been popular with holidaymakers. It has everything to offer: golden beaches, dramatic mountain scenery, golf courses, water sports and the opportunity to take time out from the 'real' world.

The busiest time of year on the island is the Glasgow Fair, two weeks in July when, traditionally, the tradesmen of the city down tools and head off for a fortnight of leisure. More distant shores may beckon for many Glaswegians on holiday these days, but there are still plenty of people for whom Arran is the best place to go: not too far away, but a complete change from the traffic and chaos of the city. Glaswegians, of course, are not the only ones who holiday on Arran. Visitors from all over the world come to revel in its beauties nowadays.

In 1889 the thought of a holiday on the west coast of Scotland was an exciting prospect for a young man from London. Nothing could be more different from life in England's capital city. Clean air, outdoor activities, money to spend and the opportunity to make new friends and acquaintances. Edwin Rose, a thirty-two-year-old office clerk, had been looking forward to his holiday for a long time. He was going to stay at the Glenburn Hydropathic in Rothesay on the Isle of Bute, with a friend, the Reverend Gustavus Goodman. Although he would be based in Rothesay, Edwin planned to make the most of his visit to Scotland, taking a few trips here and there while on holiday. He was very keen, for example, to go to Arran.

At the same time as Edwin Rose settled into the Hydro, another young man was taking up residence in humbler lodgings on Bute. This was John Watson Laurie, a twenty-six-year-old pattern-maker from Coatbridge who now lived in Glasgow. Laurie was not quite the same sort of eager, happy-go-lucky holidaymaker as Edwin Rose. He was travelling under an assumed identity – that of John Annandale – and he had newly printed business cards bearing this name tucked in his case, ready to present to anyone who asked. Later he was to claim that he had come to Bute to try to win back his former sweetheart, who had been lured from his arms by the attentions of another. In spite of this, he was quite willing to be distracted from his heartbroken mission when he made the acquaintance of Edwin Rose.

Rose and Laurie met on the steamer to Arran, the *Ivanhoe*, when they were both going on a day trip to the island. Rose was gregarious and friendly and soon struck up an amicable conversation with Laurie. Rose, having packed carefully for his holiday, was all dressed up for the outing, complete with a smart dark brown blazer and a white yachting cap. He probably seemed a little wealthier than he was. Laurie would be impressed – perhaps a little jealous. Nonetheless, Rose seemed happily oblivious to any social difference there might have been between the two of them. He was far too nice to be a snob. By the end of the day the two men had agreed that they should return to Arran together the following morning and stay for a few days. Rose wanted to do some climbing and looked forward to the challenge of Goatfell, the highest peak on the island. Laurie had very kindly found lodgings for them both (not without some difficulty, for it was high season) in a small room attached to a boarding house owned by Mrs Walker in Invercloy. There was only one bed, but the two men could squeeze in reasonably comfortably. Laurie, as he had been the one to book the room and was proposing to stay longer (until the following Saturday, he said), could have his meals prepared for him at Mrs

Walker's. Rose, who intended staying only until the Wednesday, would have to eat out, but he did not mind at all. There was Wooley's Tea-room very close at hand and that would do him nicely.

That night, back on Bute, Rose and Laurie celebrated their new-found friendship at the Glenburn Hydro in the company of two other acquaintances of Rose, William Thom and Francis Mickel, who were visiting from Linlithgow. Thom and Mickel did not take to Laurie as Rose had done. They could recognise an affected accent when they heard one, and they detected something distinctly shifty in Laurie's manner. He was a fraud and they knew it.

On Saturday 13 July Rose and Laurie sailed on the *Ivanhoe* back to Arran, Rose brimming with excitement at the thought of what lay ahead. Thom and Mickel were travelling to Arran on the same steamer, but they did not share Rose's enthusiasm for his new friend at all. They were in Arran for only two days. During that time, they caught Rose in a quiet moment and urged him to rethink his plans for the next few days. Rose seemed surprised at this, but Mickel and Thom insisted that he would be better deserting his new companion. This man 'Annandale' was a bad lot, they assured him. It would be safer to leave him well alone.

Thom and Mickel thought they had persuaded Rose to abandon his plans for the climbing expedition and leave the island, but on 15 July, as they were about to board the ferry leaving Arran, Rose came to see them off. He was, once again, all dressed up – overdressed, in fact, given the season. Kitted out in tweeds, waterproofs and complete with a walking stick, Rose was all ready to climb Goatfell. Laurie, or rather 'Annandale', was with him. Reluctantly, and with a strong sense of misgiving, Thom and Mickel left the island without Rose.

It was 3.30 p.m. when the eager Englishman and his Scottish chum set off. Goatfell has always been popular with hill-walkers, as although it is high there is a reasonably safe climb to the summit that does not present many difficulties to those who are fit. Several people noticed Rose and Laurie as they made their way up the hill-side. Laurie, acting as guide, walked in front and seemed strangely silent and preoccupied. Rose on the other hand was friendly to those whom they met, greeting them with a hearty wave and a cheerful word or two.

Strangely, although Rose and Laurie were noticed by various people both on their ascent and at the top of the mountain as they paused to take in the spectacular view, no one saw them coming back down together. At about 9 p.m., however, Laurie was seen trudging wearily down Glen Sannox. He was quite alone. He took himself for a swift drink at the Corrie Hotel before continuing his journey. He had six more miles to go, he told the landlord, for he was heading for Brodick on foot.

Mrs Walker in the boarding house at Invercloy saw nothing of her two lodgers again. Laurie, or 'Annandale' as Mrs Walker knew him, left the island, without settling his bill, by the early ferry the next day. He had with him his own luggage and Rose's as well. Laurie did not go far, however. He returned to Bute to use up the remaining days of his holiday. He was seen there, and recognised, sporting a natty yachting cap strikingly similar to the one that Edwin Rose had worn.

So what had happened to Edwin Rose?

Rose had died on the slopes of Goatfell on 15 July. It was not until 18 July, however, that people became concerned. Rose did not return to London to his waiting relatives as planned. They knew this was out of character. They contacted the Reverend Gustavus Goodman. Some days later, he replied that he had traced Rose to Mrs Walker's boarding house but could not find out what had happened to him after that. The story of the unpaid bill at the boarding house, combined with Rose's and Annandale's disappearance, had left him feeling very disturbed and he had contacted the police on Arran. Rose's father made the journey up from London as soon as he could. Something was very far wrong.

As the police investigation got under way, the newspapers took up the story of Rose's disappearance. Search parties combed the area around Goatfell and the mountain itself, but it was not until 4 August that the body of Edwin Rose was found. Two hundred people were now out looking. It was the smell that alerted Francis Logan, one of the searchers, to the spot on the hillside where Rose lay. His body was in a hollow, face down, with a large boulder on top of it. Smaller stones and bits of moss and heather had been stacked up around it. Not too far away, the searchers found Rose's cap, folded up and tucked under a stone in a stream. His waterproof coat, no longer dashing but torn and dirty, and his walking stick were also lying quite close to where the body was found. All the dead man's pockets were empty. His face was terribly smashed up.

Rose's injuries might have been consistent with a fall, but why had he been so carefully covered up? Who was the mysterious 'Annandale' with whom Rose had set off up the mountain and where was he now? If he was innocent of any part in the death of Rose, why had he not come forward to report the accident? If he had not known of the accident, then why had he not reported Rose's disappearance?

By the time Rose's body had been found, the police in Glasgow had already discovered the true identity of Annandale. Laurie had been a little too quick to make use of the contents of Rose's suitcase and his eagerness was to be his undoing.

Laurie might have hoped that his assumed identity and the false address that he had given to the landladies on both Bute and Arran would have kept the police from his door on his return to Glasgow. But someone had realised who Annandale was. If you came from the Glasgow area and you visited Rothesay or Arran during the Glasgow Fair, there was every chance that you would meet someone whom you knew. This is exactly what had happened to John Watson Laurie. He had been seen in the company of Edwin Rose on the ferry to Arran by a man called James Aitken, who knew him quite well. Laurie had been alone for a moment when Aitken had spoken to him and Laurie had told him that his companion was an Englishman and went by the name of Rose. Some days later, Aitken had seen Laurie again, back in Rothesay. It was Aitken who had noticed that Laurie was wearing a distinctive white yachting cap identical to the one that the Englishman had been wearing.

At that point Aitken had merely noticed Laurie's hat and then thought no more about it. But then Aitken met Laurie again, quite by chance, at the end of July in Glasgow. By this time the story of the missing Englishman on Arran had hit the papers and Aitken was beginning to have his suspicions. Aitken questioned Laurie about Rose and about the yachting cap. Laurie blustered a bit and made his excuses to pass on, promising that he would meet Aitken later to talk about it. He did not turn up at the appointed time, needless to say. Aitken hesitated not a moment longer. He made his way to the police station and told them what he knew.

The police now knew that they were looking for John Watson Laurie, not Mr Annandale. And they were now looking for him to question him, not about a missing person but about a very suspicious death.

Laurie, meanwhile, had realised his predicament and was already on the run. He had left his place of employment, sold his tools and packed up his belongings at his lodgings in Frederick Street.

Post-mortem examination of the body of Edwin Rose revealed that his injuries were more consistent with several hard blows to the head and face than with a fall. The newspapers reporting the story certainly made it clear what they thought. John Watson Laurie was responsible for Rose's death and must be found. The hunt was stepped up. It was now a murder inquiry.

Bizarrely, Laurie could not quite manage to lie low enough. He felt moved to write to the *North British Daily Mail*, protesting his innocence and threatening suicide. The letter was postmarked in Liverpool and the police moved in. They were too late to catch

Laurie there, however, because by the time they had tracked him down he had moved on again. All that was left for them to find were some shirts that had once belonged to Edwin Rose. Laurie had stamped his own name over the laundry marks.

On 17 August Laurie sent another letter to the newspaper, this time from Aberdeen, still protesting his innocence both of theft and of murder.

Laurie was finally caught on 3 September, by which time he had moved again, to Lanarkshire. He was spotted and chased to a wood near Hamilton. When his pursuers finally caught up with him, he had made a half-hearted attempt to cut his own throat with a razor.

The trial of John Watson Laurie began on 8 November 1889 at the High Court in Edinburgh. He admitted theft but strenuously maintained his innocence when it came to the murder charge. The jury was not entirely convinced, and they returned only a majority verdict of guilty. When the verdict was announced, Laurie's defence team swung into action with a claim that he was insane. If they were not successful, Laurie would hang in Greenock Prison on 30 November. But they were in with a chance. There was a history of mental illness in Laurie's family.

Laurie was extremely lucky. The reprieve was granted at the very last minute. A temporary stay of execution was granted by the Secretary of State for Scotland just two days before the execution date. Then, on 1 December, Laurie's sentence was commuted to life imprisonment. He was sent to Perth Prison, from where he was transferred to Peterhead. In 1893 he managed to escape from Peterhead, but his freedom was short-lived and he was recaptured and locked up again. In 1910 he was transferred back to Perth, to the asylum for the criminally insane attached to the prison. By this time Laurie was clearly losing his mind, whatever his mental state might have been in the past. He died in 1930 in the asylum, aged sixty-nine. He never confessed to the killing of Edwin Rose.

THE MYSTERY OF ARDLAMONT

The story started with a shooting. On 9 August 1893 a young man called Cecil Hambrough was shot at Ardlamont on Loch Fyne. First reports of the incident made it out to be nothing more than a tragic accident. Cecil Hambrough had been visiting a friend, Mr Monson, who had hired the place for the shooting season. The men had gone out shooting, and Hambrough had been climbing over a wall when the shotgun he was carrying had gone off accidentally. Mr Monson was, by all accounts, absolutely distraught at his friend's death. Hambrough had been alone when the accident had happened. It was Monson who had come across the tragic scene.

Initially the police were quite confident that Hambrough's death had been an accident, but there were some who felt a strange sense of uneasiness about the incident. There was mention of an insurance man whom Monson was expecting to call at Ardlamont. Gradually, uneasiness turned to suspicion. The authorities felt moved to take things further, and soon the police were back at the house at Ardlamont and the premises were being searched. Documents were removed that were pertinent to the case. Mr Monson was arrested on the charge of murdering Cecil Hambrough. It turned out that two days before Hambrough's death, Monson had insured the young man's life for £20,000.

Gradually the details of the people who were involved in the tragedy at Ardlamont emerged. Cecil Hambrough was not so much a friend of Mr Monson as his charge. Hambrough's father, a somewhat impecunious major with high hopes for his son, had engaged Monson as a gentleman tutor for Cecil. He had engaged Monson on account of his gentleman's credentials rather than for his impeccable references. Major Hambrough knew very little about Monson. He certainly did not know that despite being well connected Monson was in severe financial difficulties. Monson had already claimed a large amount of insurance money once before when a house that he had rented had mysteriously burnt to the ground. He had also been arrested on suspicion of fraud on another occasion, although nothing had been proved against him. When he met the Hambroughs, Monson was in desperate financial straits and about to become bankrupt.

Monson saw no harm in taking the young Cecil under his wing. He had been promised a good fee in return for his services after all. Any money in his pocket was a bonus. As time went by and life was getting progressively more difficult for Monson and his wife in Yorkshire (bankruptcy can have that effect), they packed up and left for Scotland, taking up residence at Ardlamont. Cecil Hambrough went with them.

Monson was able to conceal his financial difficulties once he was north of the border with astonishing ease. Convincing all those whom he met that he was a well-connected and wealthy Englishman, he was able to take over the estate at Ardlamont for the shooting season without handing over so much as a penny and to settle down with his family to enjoy some seriously splendid living with servants, good food and fine wines. His unwitting pupil, Cecil, blissfully unaware that his days were numbered, probably thought that things could not be better. Here he was, in beautiful surroundings, having a thoroughly good time. As the onset of the shooting season approached, four of his comrades were due to join him (for a fee, naturally, payable to Monson). It would be such fun.

The wheelings and dealings that had gone on behind the scenes prior to the Monsons' removal to Ardlamont were complicated to say the least and were to challenge the minds of the jury considerably when Monson was brought to trial.

Monson was to be tried on two counts: one of attempted murder and one of murder. The charge of attempted murder was brought against Monson after police discovered that on 9 August Cecil Hambrough had come quite close to losing his life in another suspicious incident, out on the loch.

The story is very complicated but can be understood better if events are taken in chronological order, starting in Yorkshire, with Monson recently given charge of Cecil Hambrough before he made his plans for his move to Scotland to make life a little easier for himself.

Monson was declared bankrupt shortly after taking charge of Cecil. He was living in Harrogate at the time, but Harrogate was becoming a little uncomfortable for him; he had always lived on credit and now he could not get it anywhere. So he moved to Riseley Hall, a grand and generously proportioned house some distance away. Undeterred by his financial predicament, he established his family there with a full retinue of servants and lived the high life to the full for as long as it was possible. After things became too difficult at Riseley Hall – one can only survive on huge amounts of credit for so long in one place – Monson prepared to move the family again, this time to Scotland, borrowing the cost of the removal, almost certainly without the slightest intention of paying the loan back. By this time, Cecil's father, the Major, had become completely disenchanted with Monson and had urged his son to leave his tutor's care. But Cecil was quite happy where he was. It must be said that the young man cannot have been very bright. He must have been aware to some extent of Monson's precarious situation. Nonetheless, his tutor was a charismatic and persuasive man, and in spite of everything had so far been able to provide Cecil with a most comfortable and amusing lifestyle for three years. His father, on the other hand, could provide little more for him than dingy digs in London. Cecil ignored his father's protestations and stayed right where he was.

Monson had no money. He was in considerable debt. As long as one month before Cecil Hambrough met his end at Ardlamont, Monson had begun to try to take out a life assurance policy on the life of his pupil for a massive amount of money. He tried one or two insurance companies, telling them that he wanted a policy drawn up on the life of Cecil Hambrough in his wife's name. Initially his efforts were unsuccessful. Gradually, he reduced the amount that Cecil's life was to be assured for and invented a fine story as to why the young man's life should be assured so heavily. He told the insurance company that Cecil was about to inherit a huge amount of money. Cecil had expressed an interest in buying the estate at Ardlamont, and to this end, Monson claimed, Mrs Monson was advancing the young man the sum of £20,000. Mrs Monson would need the assurance policy on Cecil's life to cover this amount until Cecil came into his inheritance. Needless to say, none of this was true. But Cecil, ever the compliant pupil, was quite easily persuaded to sign the necessary papers. By the time it had all been arranged, and Monson had assembled enough money (through fraudulent means, naturally) to pay the assurance premium, it was 8 August and they were settled in the house at Ardlamont.

Another character entered the scene on the same day. Edward Sweeney, a bookie from London and an acquaintance of Monson's, joined the party at Ardlamont. Just exactly what part he was to play in the events of the next couple of days will never be known. Edward Sweeney slipped away into temporary obscurity after the shooting and was never questioned by police, but his presence was undoubtedly suspicious. He turned up at Ardlamont, at Monson's invitation, under an assumed name and identity – that of Edward Scott, engineer.

'Scott' was present at both incidents for which Monson was being tried. He may have been an accessory – he may have been hired to do the dirty work – nothing can be proved now. But if he had nothing to feel guilty about, then why did he come to Ardlamont under an assumed name and why did he leave so swiftly?

The first incident – for which Monson was charged with attempted murder – took place on 9 August. Monson and Scott had borrowed a small boat. That evening, Monson proposed a fishing expedition on the loch to Cecil Hambrough. Cecil was happy to take part. The boat had not gone far out into the loch, however, when it began to fill up with water and within minutes both Monson and his pupil were in the water with the upturned boat beside them. Monson was a competent swimmer and, although obviously very wet, was completely unconcerned by the incident. Cecil Hambrough, however, who could not swim (and we might assume that Monson knew this), considered himself very fortunate that the boat had not yet reached the deeper waters of the loch and that he was able to make his way ashore without too much difficulty. It had been a close thing.

The police investigating Hambrough's death came to hear of this incident and examined the boat that had been taken out for the trip. A hole had been cut in the bottom of the boat – a hole such as might be used for drainage purposes, which ought to be corked when the boat was on the water. But this hole had no cork and had been newly cut. It seemed reasonable to assume that the sinking boat on the loch had been Monson's first attempt at staging an 'accident' for Hambrough. The plan had backfired only because the boat had capsized before they reached deep water.

At the time of the incident Monson made light of it, and the party retired to the house for a stiff drink or two. They had plenty more fun to look forward to.

The second incident took place the next morning. Monson, Hambrough and Scott set off early in the morning for a spot of shooting. Monson had borrowed a larger gun than usual for the occasion – did he have big game in mind?

At first Monson's version of the events that took place after that were accepted at face value by the investigating authorities. According to Monson, the three men went their separate ways once they got into the woods. Cecil Hambrough had been alone when he had shot himself. It was a terrible accident. The gun must have gone off when he was climbing over the dyke where he was found. Scott's version of events would never be heard by the police. He left, immediately after the incident. By the time the police realised that there was more to the incident than they had first thought, he was well away. A warrant was issued for his arrest and a description of him was published, but all efforts to track him down and bring him to trial with Monson were fruitless.

The members of the jury had their work cut out for them as they tried to absorb the mass of evidence that was presented to them in court. The prosecution went to great lengths to try to establish that Cecil Hambrough could not have shot himself in the manner that was claimed. They also brought forward evidence that trees near to the scene of Hambrough's death had been scarred by gunshot. This was proof, they claimed, that someone had been shooting at the young man from a distance.

There were arguments from the defence to counter both these proposals. First of all, it could not be proved beyond doubt that it was physically impossible for the wounds that Hambrough had suffered to have been caused accidentally. Secondly, the defence maintained that the woods where Cecil Hambrough died were in constant use for shooting and that the trees could have been marked by gunshot at any time.

But the crucial argument for the defence rested on the £20,000 assurance policy on Cecil Hambrough's life. Monson had taken the policy out not in his own name but in his wife's name. Legally, Mrs Monson was the one who would benefit if it was paid out. There was absolutely no proof that Mr Monson himself stood to gain directly from Cecil Hambrough's death. Of course, Mr Monson was married to Mrs Monson, and she might well be persuaded to be generous with her insurance money should she get it. But that was not the point. Strictly speaking Mr Monson had no claim on it and thus did not stand to gain from it. Monson was a clever chap!

The judge gave weight to the defence's arguments in his summing up before the jury went out to consider their verdict:

> It is the business of the crown to prove the case, not for the defence to prove innocence.

The case had caused a sensation. It is very likely that many, if not most, of the people who were in court to hear all the evidence that was presented believed that Monson had killed his young charge, in all probability with the help of the elusive Scott, but in the end the case for the defence had won the day. The jury returned with a verdict of 'not proven'.

The verdict of not proven is unique to Scots law and is unpopular with many solicitors and advocates. It leaves a lingering doubt in the air: the innocent have not been declared innocent and the guilty may go free. Monson walked free, but the doubt lingers still, long after his death.

The firm of solicitors who represented Monson when he went for trial, Davidson and Syme, used to have their offices in a building in Edinburgh's Charlotte Square. The building is now the headquarters of the National Trust for Scotland. Two small but significant items have been donated to the Trust to display in the building: a gold cigar-cutter and a silver pocket watch. These were given to his solicitors by Monson as security for his legal costs; they remained undisturbed in the firm's safe for many years. Now they will go on show as interesting curiosities; another of Monson's many unpaid debts and a testament to the sheer nerve of the man.

THE MURDER OF MARION GILCHRIST AND THE TRIALS OF OSCAR SLATER

There are two victims in this murder story. The first was the victim of a terrible crime. The second was the victim of gross injustice, brought about by a lethal cocktail of over-zealous policing, a disregard for sound investigative procedure and undoubtedly social, religious and racial prejudice.

Oscar Slater was born in Germany, the son of a baker and his wife. The family were Jewish. Oscar found various kinds of gainful employment as he grew towards adulthood, but when the time came for him to serve his duty in the armed forces, he decided that conscription was not for him and left Germany before he was sent his papers. He entered the world of gambling in London after he got a job working for a bookie and was soon wheeling and dealing in his own right, organising gambling circles and buying and selling the odd piece of jewellery. He moved to Glasgow, where he met and married a Scots girl. The marriage was a mistake: his wife drank heavily and became such a torment that Oscar left her. Unfortunately, the woman proved to be more tenacious than Oscar had anticipated. Whenever he tried to shake her off, she tracked him down. He was forced to adopt false names in order to put her off the scent.

Oscar eventually moved back to London, where he became

attached to Madame Andrée Junio Antoine, a working woman who entertained her other 'gentlemen clients' when Oscar was out conducting his own business. The pair travelled to the United States together – Oscar had visited the country a few times before – and spent a successful year helping to run a gambling club in New York. They returned to Britain in 1908, first to London and then to Glasgow. Oscar's alias was now Adolf Anderson. Oscar and his mistress went back to their former patterns of work quite happily. Oscar was generally out wheeling and dealing all day while Madame Antoine received her clients. In the evenings, Oscar usually returned home for dinner, which the couple ate together.

Oscar Slater was hardly a criminal. He was an entrepreneur, a speculator whose dealings might not have been entirely legitimate, but he was not a hard man, nor a thief. There can be little doubt that he did not deserve what lay in store for him in 1908 after his return to Glasgow.

Marion Gilchrist was a spinster. She lived in a flat on the first floor of a tenement building in West Princes Street, Glasgow. She did not live alone: she had a live-in maid, named Nellie Lambie. Miss Gilchrist was comfortably off and had a considerable amount of valuable jewellery hidden in various secret places around the flat. She was very much aware that a woman in her position was a likely prey to thieves. She kept her front door firmly locked at all times, whether she was in or out of the flat. Three locks in total were used to secure the door. Two of the locks were used at all times, the third was only locked when Miss Gilchrist went to bed at night. Downstairs, the close door that led on to the street was usually kept locked as well, for added security. Any likely thief would certainly have his work cut out for him if he wanted to break into the home of Marion Gilchrist.

In the flat immediately below Miss Gilchrist lived the Adams family. Their front door opened onto the street, next to the door for the stair, or close, where Marion Gilchrist's flat was. The

Adams family consisted of Mrs Adams and her son Arthur and his two sisters.

On 21 December 1908, Arthur Adams was in the dining room of his flat with his sisters, making preparations for Christmas, when they heard some strange noises coming from the flat above. This was unusual; one of the benefits of having an elderly lady as an upstairs neighbour was that there were no problems with noise from above. The noises consisted of a loud thump, followed by three knocks. The Adams family knew Miss Gilchrist and were aware that she was nervous; she had even elicited from them a promise that, should they hear her knocking on the floor, they were to take it as a signal from her that something was wrong and come to her aid. Arthur Adams was sufficiently concerned when he heard the thumps from upstairs that night to stop what he was doing and go and investigate.

The first thing that Adams noticed was the door of the close. It was unlocked. This was certainly unusual. Adams climbed the stairs to the first floor and rang Miss Gilchrist's front doorbell. When he peered through the glass in the front door he could see that a light was on in the hallway. It looked as if someone was in, so when he got no reply the first time, he rang the bell once again, this time with considerably more force. He could hear sounds of activity coming from the flat now: it sounded like someone chopping sticks for the fire. Deciding that the noise was probably just that – Nellie Lambie chopping kindling for her mistress's living-room fire, too absorbed in her task to hear the doorbell – Arthur went back downstairs and returned to his own flat.

His sisters, however, were quite insistent that something was very much wrong in the flat upstairs; they had never heard noises like that before. They sent Arthur back to try the doorbell one more time. He went back up to Miss Gilchrist's front door, rang the bell very loudly and waited. Just then, there were footsteps on the stairs and Nellie Lambie, Miss Gilchrist's maid, arrived on the landing behind him. She had been out on an errand for her mistress. Arthur, now aware that the noises that he had heard through the door a moment or two ago could not have been the sounds of Nellie chopping firewood, told her of his concerns. Nellie dismissed them as nothing. The pulley that was used for drying clothes in the kitchen was making a dreadful noise, she said. It needed oiling. It was probably the pulley that the Adams family had heard. But the noises had come from Miss Gilchrist's dining room, which was directly above the Adams' dining room. They had not come from the kitchen. Arthur Adams still felt that he ought to linger long enough to ensure that all was well with Miss Gilchrist.

Nellie Lambie unlocked the front door and the two of them went into the hall. Nellie headed straight for the kitchen, which was situated on the left-hand side of the hall, but just as she did so, a man appeared from another room – a bedroom – on the right-hand side. He had the appearance of quite a respectable gentleman and, strangely, Nellie Lambie was apparently unperturbed by his presence in the flat. If she was surprised to find him there, she certainly did not show it. To Arthur Adams, it seemed as if she recognised him. The man came towards Arthur Adams, paused as if to say something, then suddenly brushed past him and headed at full speed for the stairs. Nellie, meanwhile, went into the kitchen to have a look at the pulley. She came out again to say that everything was all right, but Arthur Adams had other concerns. Where was Miss Gilchrist? Nellie then went into the dining room to look for her mistress. She screamed at what she saw in there. Arthur Adams followed her in. He too, gasped at what he saw. Miss Gilchrist lay in a pool of blood in front of the dining room fire. A rug had been hastily flung over her head.

Arthur Adams at once tried to give chase to the man who had met them when they arrived in the flat. He left Nellie to summon help and ran downstairs and out into the street. When he got outside, he ran some distance down West Princes Street, but saw no one in the darkness. He ran back in the other direction and peered along the street as far as he could see. All that he saw were some figures far in the distance – too far for him to catch up with. He went back up to Miss Gilchrist's flat. By this time a policeman had arrived. They carefully uncovered Miss Gilchrist and found that she was still breathing, although she was obviously close to death. Arthur ran for the doctor – Dr Adams (no relation), who lived close by – but by the time the doctor arrived in the flat to examine Miss Gilchrist, she was dead. A chair lay by her side, covered in bloodstains. This, the doctor declared, had in all likelihood been the murder weapon.

The policeman called for the detective squad, and they arrived soon afterwards to search the flat for evidence and question the witnesses. Naturally, they were interested in the stranger who had been in the flat when Nellie had let Arthur Adams in. Arthur Adams had not been in a position to see the man very clearly, for he had not had his spectacles on at the time, but he told the police what he knew. The man was quite young – probably in his late twenties or early thirties. He was slim, dark and clean-shaven. He was wearing a light-coloured overcoat and a cloth cap, which was darker in colour. He was about five feet nine inches tall.

Nellie told the police that she had hardly seen the man. She also told them that she had been out of the flat for no more than ten minutes or so. She had only stepped out to get a paper for Miss Gilchrist. This meant that if the stranger had not been in the flat before she left – and it appeared that this was the case – he had not had much time in which to act.

The search of the flat revealed the following.

A gas lamp had been lit in a spare bedroom in Nellie Lambie's absence. Beneath the lamp was a table on which the police found a box of matches that were not the kind that were used in the flat. The table also had on it a toilet dish with some jewellery in it and a wooden box that had contained some papers. There was also a gold pocket watch and chain. The wooden box had been forced open and its contents lay scattered on the floor beneath the table. Strangely, the jewellery had, for the most part, been left well alone. The only thing that was missing, according to Nellie Lambie, was a brooch. The brooch was quite distinctive: crescent-shaped and decorated with diamonds.

Perhaps the murderer was prevented from taking anything else by the arrival of Nellie Lambie and Arthur Adams, but the jewellery had been quite accessible on the table. Could he not have grabbed a handful of trinkets, or at least the watch and chain, before he made his getaway?

There was no sign of a forced entry to the flat. Miss Gilchrist had been very wary of strangers. It was most unlikely that she would have let anyone into her flat, especially as she was alone, unless she knew him. The police, therefore, concentrated their questioning on Nellie Lambie. Could the killer have been a friend of Miss Gilchrist or a friend of Nellie Lambie?

It was at this point that the case began to go wrong. One promising young detective, John Trench, was sure that Nellie Lambie had known the man who had appeared in the hallway that night. He was someone with whom both she and Miss Gilchrist were familiar. This crucial fact was later to be ignored by the officers in charge of the investigation. The fact that she had hardly seen him was given greater weight instead, as the investigation moved on in the coming days and began to centre on a man called Oscar Slater.

A second description, of a man who was said to have been seen running from the entrance to Miss Gilchrist's close, was given to the police. It did not quite match the description given by the myopic Arthur Adams. Police published both descriptions in case there was more than one man involved in the killing, but the details that differed may not have been as crucial as the police thought. The girl who gave the second description, Mary Barrowman, provided a little more detail than Adams had done.

She described the stranger as tall, while Adams had said that he was about five feet nine inches in height. We do not know how tall Mary Barrowman was, but she was only fourteen years old. She was probably not yet fully grown. Five feet nine inches might have seemed quite tall to a young girl of smaller stature. Mary described the stranger's overcoat as a light fawn waterproof. Adams thought it was light grey. The two colours are not hugely dissimilar, and we should remember that Adams saw the man inside while Mary Barrowman claimed to have seen him outside in the darkened street. The light would be different, as would one's perception of colour.

On Christmas Day, a man who had read of the murder in the papers and had seen both descriptions of the man and wanted to help the police with their inquiries, came forward with some information. The man was a member of a club in India Street, where a man called Oscar was also a member. Oscar had been trying to find a buyer amongst the other club members for a pawn ticket that he had. The ticket was for a crescent-shaped diamond brooch. He knew where Oscar lived – 69 St George's Road.

Oscar Slater, a German Jew, seemed like a very credible suspect to the police. Their investigations revealed that he was a gambler – hardly a respectable profession and one likely to lead to financial difficulties. Slater was also known to buy and sell jewellery. The transactions he made were not quite the same as those that were made in high street jewellers' shops. They were much more private. Perhaps they were a little shady. The police discovered that Slater lived with a woman known as Madame Andrée Junio Antoine, who was not exactly a model of respectability herself. Slater also used aliases; the name at the door of his house was that of A. Anderson, dentist.

It was all looking quite promising as the police made their way to 69 St George's Road to pay a visit to Oscar Slater. When they got to the house, they found that Slater and his mistress had both left. Slater's maid told them that they had gone on Christmas Day, headed for America. A shady lifestyle, a pawn ticket, a sudden departure. Oscar's prospects were looking bleaker and bleaker.

Then the police managed to trace the brooch that Oscar Slater had pawned. It was decorated with diamonds, it was crescent-shaped, but there the similarity ended. It was most definitely not the brooch that had been taken from Miss Gilchrist's house, and Oscar Slater had pawned it long before Miss Gilchrist's death.

By rights, the police ought to have stopped pursuing Oscar Slater right there and then. Apart from the chance that the brooch might have been Miss Gilchrist's, they had nothing whatsoever to establish a link between Slater and the killing. They had no real reason to suspect him any more. Oscar Slater might have been a bit of a dodgy character, but he was not a known thief, nor did he have a reputation as a violent man. There were hundreds of other dodgy characters in Glasgow, just like him. Why should Oscar Slater be the one who had killed Miss Gilchrist?

The police would not let go. Slater had left for America quite suddenly. He was running from something, they decided; in all probability, he was running from a murder charge.

Oscar and his mistress had sailed on the *Lusitania* to New York. When it docked in early January, police met Slater and Madame Junio Antoine as they disembarked. Both were arrested and incarcerated. A search of their luggage revealed that Oscar Slater was in possession of a light-coloured raincoat, which was stained – could it be blood from the murder? There was also a small tool set in the luggage, including a small hammer. This, the police decided, was the murder weapon. They were forgetting (or choosing to overlook) the bloodstained chair that had been found beside Miss Gilchrist's body.

Oscar Slater had not left suddenly for America in fact. He had spent some three weeks in preparation for his travels, making arrangements with a friend who lived in the United States for his journey to San Francisco and finding another tenant to take up the lease on his flat. He did bring the date of travel forward by some days when he found out that his troublesome wife was yet again on his trail, but when it came to packing up and leaving on Christmas night, his preparations were unhurried and careful and his luggage beautifully organised – hardly the behaviour of a man on the run for murder.

Meanwhile, back in Britain, Oscar Slater's picture appeared in the papers. A reward had already been offered for information that might lead to the conviction of Miss Gilchrist's murderer – £200, quite a tidy sum. After Slater's picture appeared in the papers, there were suddenly plenty of people who felt quite confident that they could recognise this man. Oscar Slater, according to the willing witnesses who came forward, had been seen near Miss Gilchrist's flat before, after and on the day of her murder.

Slater had to be extradited from the United States before any further action could be taken against him in Scotland. To this end, arrangements were made to pay for the passage of Mary Barrowman, Nellie Lambie and Arthur Adams to New York. Further repeated questioning sessions by police had been quite skilful and by now the descriptions of the man that Nellie Lambie and Mary Barrowman had seen were almost identical. These two 'independent' witnesses were, strangely, given a cabin to share on the voyage. When the three witnesses were taken to the identification parade, it was quite clear which man of the three before them they were supposed to pick. He was handcuffed to another man, who was far too tall to be a likely suspect. The other man, free of bonds, could not be the one the police were holding in custody. Whatever they might have thought, it was obvious to the three witnesses that they were supposed to pick out Oscar Slater. So they did, albeit with some hesitation, for Slater was neither of slim build nor clean-shaven. He was short and broad and had a moustache. Nor was he aged between twenty-five and thirty. He was thirty-seven years old and could not have passed for a younger man. The American authorities were not happy with the identification, and the lawyer who was representing Slater urged him to continue to fight against the extradition.

But Slater felt he had nothing to fear. If he went back to Scotland, he could clear his name without difficulty. He ought to have been right. He had a strong alibi for 21 December, the night of the murder. (At this point, however, he was more concerned about his alibi for 22 December, the night after the murder – for so little did Oscar Slater know of the crime of which he was being accused that he thought that the murder had taken place on the 22nd.)

If all had been fair at his subsequent trial, Slater's innocence could have been proved beyond reasonable doubt. His alibi for the night of 21 December, however, was never brought up in court. All was not fair. Moreover, there were, unbeknown to him, all those willing witnesses waiting for him back in Scotland; witnesses whose eyes must have been gleaming at the thought of a £200 reward.

Oscar Slater sailed back to Britain under escort, ready to prove his innocence, sadly unprepared for his assumed guilt. Before he left for Scotland, at this point still believing that Marion Gilchrist had been killed on the night of 22 December, he wrote to a friend back in Scotland asking for support and stressing that he could find five men to support his alibi for that night.

If Oscar Slater had committed the murder, then why was he putting all his efforts into proving his whereabouts on the wrong night? The day one commits murder is surely not one so easily forgotten. This fact, like so many others crucial to the case, was to be ignored. Back in Glasgow another identification parade awaited.

This time Oscar was placed in a line with some policemen in plain clothes and some railway officials. Bear in mind that Oscar was a foreigner – and he looked foreign. The men with whom he was placed in the identification parade were all quite obviously British.

In addition to this, thanks to the attention the press had given to the case, the witnesses had all had a chance to have a good look at Slater's photograph in the paper. They were probably well prepared to identify someone who looked like the photograph in the paper rather than the man they claimed to have seen hanging around Marion Gilchrist's house – if they had seen a man at all. Could there have been any possibility of any of the witnesses pointing to the wrong man and announcing: 'That's him!'?

And so to the trial, which took place in Edinburgh, beginning on 3 May 1909. The people had waited a long time for this. By now the tide of opinion had well and truly turned against Slater. In theory he should have been presumed innocent until proven guilty. In reality, Oscar Slater's defence team found themselves facing an uphill task trying to prove that he was innocent. He was, quite definitely, assumed to be guilty. Whatever doubts the prosecution lawyers had about the strength of their case against Oscar Slater, they did not show them in court. The man appearing for the prosecution was none other than the Lord Advocate himself, Alexander Ure. A skilful and persuasive advocate,he was determined to get his man, by fair means or foul.

Mr A. McClure, appearing for Slater, did a good job as far as it went, but he omitted to bring up certain points that were crucial to the case. Firstly, Oscar Slater had an alibi for the night of the murder. Miss Gilchrist had been killed at around seven o'clock in the evening. At that time, according to both Slater's mistress and his maid, Slater had returned home, as he usually did, to eat dinner. He had stayed at home for more than an hour. He had witnesses who testified to his presence in various places during the afternoon before the murder. His last port of call had been a billiard hall in Renfield Street. He had left there at six-thirty. The prosecution claimed that it was at this point that Slater had gone to Miss Gilchrist's flat, killed her and then returned home by a very circuitous route, arriving at his flat hours later than usual. Had the defence been more efficient, they would surely have protested against this proposition. There was no time for Oscar to race all the way to Miss Gilchrist's, kill her and arrive home in time for seven o'clock. And there were witnesses who said he was home by seven o'clock. In fact, from the billiard room in Renfield Street, it was virtually impossible for Oscar to have got to Miss Gilchrist's in time to kill her. The prosecution's propositions made no real sense; they were not backed up by evidence of any sort. They were pure conjecture, but they were put with such persuasion that they won the day.

Again, the defence was to let Slater down when it came to the hours immediately after Miss Gilchrist's death. Slater had witnesses to say that he had come home for dinner. Their statements were virtually overlooked in the judge's summing up of the case. The defence plainly did not give enough weight to their statements when presenting its case – either that or the judge felt that they had been lying.

If the defence lawyers had researched the case a little more thoroughly, they might have found out about another witness, one whom the prosecution knew about, but chose not to call to give evidence for obvious reasons. This witness was a grocer to whom Oscar Slater was familiar as a customer. He saw Oscar Slater standing at the entrance to his close, smoking a cigar in a calm and relaxed fashion, at about eight-fifteen on the night of the murder. Slater certainly did not have the appearance of a man who had committed a hasty and brutal murder only an hour earlier. The grocer's statement never came to the attention of the defence and was never brought up in court. It might have saved Oscar Slater.

If we recall how security conscious the late Miss Gilchrist was, then we will be surprised that nothing was made of the fact that the means by which Oscar was supposed to have gained entry to her flat remained a mystery. The police had been convinced that she must have known her assailant. There had been no forced entry and Miss Gilchrist would never have opened her door to a stranger. This appears to have been conveniently overlooked from the moment the police fixed their attentions on Oscar Slater. The prosecution did not give any explanation as to how Slater was supposed to have become familiar with Miss Gilchrist and gained access to her home. They concentrated their line of attack on the fact that they had several witnesses who could attest to Slater's presence in the area, lurking suspiciously, in the days leading up to the murder.

Once again, the case for the prosecution did not make much sense. The Lord Advocate was very eloquent in his description of Slater, lurking, watching, making a mental note of the regular movements of the two women in Miss Gilchrist's flat. He knew when to strike.

But if this was the case, why had Oscar chosen a moment when he had only minutes to carry out the terrible deed? If he had been 'casing the joint', he would know that Nellie's trip was bound to be a short one – her usual outing to get the evening paper. If he really had been watching Miss Gilchrist's flat for as long as the prosecution claimed, then he would surely know that there were better moments to pick when he would have more time. Nellie Lambie had time off twice a week, during which she always went out. Why did Oscar not act then? Nobody asked this question.

Then there was the question of the murder weapon. Dr Adams, arriving at the scene of the murder, had declared that a chair had been used to kill Miss Gilchrist. This fact was completely overlooked when the police found the hammer in Oscar Slater's luggage. The hammer was stained and the police decided that the stains could be blood; they were, in fact, rust. But the hammer was still supposed to be the murder weapon. Dr Adams was never called to give evidence as to his findings.

Finally, there was Oscar Slater's supposed motive – a need for money. This made little sense. Oscar had enough money for his trip to the United States and he was not short of cash either. The brooch that he had pawned – the brooch that had started off the whole dismal affair – had earned him £30. He had work waiting for him in the United States. He had no need to rob Miss Gilchrist. Besides, apart from the brooch that was missing, the brooch that Oscar Slater had clearly not taken, nothing had gone from Miss Gilchrist's home. There had been plenty of valuable items lying within easy reach, items that could have been grabbed as the killer made his hasty exit, but nothing else had been taken.

The Lord Advocate was determined to have Oscar Slater found guilty and although the evidence upon which he based his case was decidedly shaky to say the least, the power of his rhetoric concealed the weaknesses in his arguments well enough to convince most of the jury. The judge, Lord Guthrie, appeared to have been convinced as well. His summing up of the case made his opinion perfectly clear. He condemned Oscar Slater as a fundamentally dishonest person of unsavoury character. He ignored the alibi that Madame Junio Antoine and Oscar's maid had given him for the evening of the murder. In short, Lord Guthrie ensured that Oscar Slater's fate was sealed.

The verdict was not unanimous. Nine found Slater guilty, five found the case against him not proven, one found him innocent. The conviction had been secured by a narrow majority, but it was enough to win the case for the prosecution. Oscar Slater was pronounced guilty as charged and sentenced to death. His dismay at the court's findings was obvious for all to see. He had not been permitted to take the stand in his own defence in case his foreign accent prejudiced his case. Now he would not be silenced. He stood up in court after the verdict had been announced and protested his innocence most forcefully. Whether this made him feel any better, we do not know. It certainly did not help him. He was to be hanged on 27 May 1909.

Immediately after the trial, the tide of public opinion began to shift in Oscar Slater's favour. Several thousand people gave their names to a petition calling for the death sentence to be commuted.

The petition argued two main points. First, it stated that Oscar Slater's character ought not to have been called into question in the way it was before the jury reached their verdict. This had prejudiced his case. Secondly, the identification of Oscar Slater had been most unsatisfactory.

Two days before he was due to be hanged, the terrified and bewildered Oscar Slater found that his sentence had been commuted to life imprisonment. He was transferred to Peterhead Prison. From there he continued to protest his innocence at every opportunity. He believed that someone, somewhere, would be able to help him. His words in a letter to Mr Shaughnessy, the lawyer whom he engaged to help him, showed that in spite of everything he still had faith that justice would win the day:

> I will fight so long as I live in here, I am not crying to get
> liberated, I want justice and this I will get at last.

There were several people on Slater's side. One of Oscar's supporters was the great Arthur Conan Doyle, who published a book on the case in August 1912. He felt that a crucial point overlooked in the investigation was the rifled box of papers in Miss Gilchrist's flat. He believed that the papers – in particular a will – held the reason for the murder. Sir Edward Marshall Hall brought the matter up in parliament, asking the Scottish Secretary to act. The Scottish Secretary did nothing.

It was fortunate for Oscar Slater that there was one man in the Glasgow police force who felt very strongly that justice had not been done. Detective-Lieutenant John Trench, who had been involved in the case from the outset, was deeply disturbed. From the very first day of the murder investigation, Trench had been given every reason to believe that Nellie Lambie had known the intruder in Miss Gilchrist's flat.

Trench had been silenced in his protestations to his superiors at the time as they were hot in pursuit of Oscar Slater, but the affair did not sit easily on his conscience. Then in 1912 Trench had become involved in another case that had borne remarkable similarities to the Gilchrist case. An elderly spinster had been murdered in her home in Broughty Ferry, and by means that could only be described as dubious the police had found several witnesses to identify a Canadian man as the likely culprit. It had been Trench who had put in the effort and the real detective work to prove that this man was entirely innocent. As he worked on the Broughty Ferry case, the Gilchrist case can never have been far from his mind. Slater's unfortunate predicament troubled him more and more.

Trench was in a difficult position. He was putting his own career at risk, calling the actions of his own police force into question, but he felt strongly that his moral duty was to speak up. He told his story to a lawyer, David Cook, and asked for his help. Through David Cook, Trench's concerns reached the ears of the Scottish Secretary. At the Scottish Secretary's request, Trench supplied him with a long and detailed document containing the information that he felt was vital to the Slater case. This move was backed up by a plea, made in March 1914 by David Cook, for the Scottish Secretary to open an inquiry into the case.

Finally the inquiry was arranged and Trench had his turn to speak. His concerns about the case were several:

1   He believed that Nellie Lambie had recognised the intruder in her mistress's flat on the night of the murder. He claimed that the police had been told the name of the man whom Nellie Lambie believed it to have been and it was not Oscar Slater.

2   He thought that the statement of Mary Barrowman, and her description of the man she claimed to have seen on the night of the murder was pure fabrication. Barrowman had said that

she was in West Princes Street on an errand on the night in question, but her employers had denied this.

3   Oscar Slater's supposed flight from justice gave cause for concern. There was remarkably little evidence to suggest that he had left in a great hurry. Moreover, upon his arrival in Liverpool he had quite openly signed his name in the hotel register as 'Oscar Slater, Glasgow'. Oscar Slater had never hesitated to use false names in the past. If he really was on the run, then why had he chosen to use his own name now, of all times? Moreover, Oscar's eventual destination, New York, and the means by which he was travelling, on board the *Lusitania*, were never a secret.

4   The matches found on the table below the gas lamp in the spare bedroom in Miss Gilchrist's house were Runaway matches. This was a brand that Miss Gilchrist did not use and the box was supposed to have been left by the killer. When Trench went to search Oscar Slater's flat he found no evidence to suggest that this particular brand of matches was used in the Slater residence either.

The most important point that Trench made concerned Nellie Lambie's supposed identification of the intruder. Trench was most insistent about this, and it cost him his job, for he was calling into question the evidence of his superiors.

Trench had become involved in the case when Central Division, to which he belonged, was called in to help Western Division. One of the first pieces of information he was given about the case was the description of the wanted man that had been supplied by Arthur Adams and Nellie Lambie.

On 22 December, Trench knew that three police officers, including Superintendent Douglas, had visited the house of a man known as A. B., following up some information that Nellie Lambie had given them.

On 23 December, Trench had gone, at the request of Chief Superintendent Orr, to take a statement from Miss Birrel, 19 Blythswood Drive. Miss Birrel was Miss Gilchrist's niece, and Nellie Lambie had visited her on the night of the murder to tell her of her aunt's death. Miss Birrel told Trench that Nellie Lambie had stated, quite categorically, that A. B. had been the man she had seen in the flat. A. B., according to Nellie Lambie, had been the murderer. Miss Birrel also said that Nellie Lambie had told the police about A. B.

Upon his return to headquarters with this information, Trench had been congratulated. According to Chief Superintendent Orr, it was 'the first real clue we have got'. Superintendent Ord was present with his superior, Orr, when Trench passed on the information. Shortly after that, Ord told Trench that he had consulted Superintendent Douglas, who was convinced that A. B. had nothing to do with the affair.

Trench had been less convinced. He visited Nellie Lambie at her aunt's house on 3 January, accompanied by Detective Keith. He showed a sketch of Oscar Slater to her, but she did not recognise him. Trench then mentioned A. B. Was that possibly the man whom she saw? Nellie's reply was: 'It's gey funny if it wasn't him I saw!' Trench then went back to Ord with this information but was more or less ignored. The intruder was not A. B., according to Ord. The matter had been 'cleared up'.

Trench's theory that Nellie Lambie had known the identity of the intruder and that the intruder had been A. B. made a great deal of sense. It explained why Nellie had shown no apparent dismay at the man's appearance. It also explained how the man had gained entry to the flat. A. B. was known both to Nellie Lambie and Miss Gilchrist.

When fellow officers in Central Division and Western Division were questioned at the inquiry, however, they were adamant to a man that Trench was not telling the truth. Trench had a copy of the statement made by Miss Birrel on 23 December, but, strangely, such a statement was missing from the file held by Superintendent Ord. Detective Keith denied that Trench had ever mentioned A. B. to Nellie Lambie on 9 January. And so it went on. If the Glasgow police had realised that their investigation was a foul-up, they certainly were not going to admit it. To add to Trench's misery, Nellie Lambie and Miss Birrel, when questioned again, denied the whole story of the mysterious A. B. The whole inquiry was a farce. It benefited Oscar Slater not one bit.

Detective-Lieutenant John Trench was suspended from duty on 14 July. His conscience had cost him his career.

In early August, war broke out and there were other things on the minds of the government and the great British public. Oscar Slater was left to languish in jail.

For Trench and Cook, the lawyer who had helped him, things were getting worse. In May 1915, both men were arrested separately on similar charges of reset. The crime had supposedly taken place in January 1914. The whole affair was clearly a set-up, with the police behind it, and luckily Trench and Cook were acquitted, but the whole affair had left them with a very bad taste in their mouths.

It was now abundantly clear that Trench could take the Slater case no further personally. He had taken up a career in the army and now he went to serve abroad.

Slater, amazingly, had still not given up hope. The years went by – five, ten, fifteen – still he was not released, but he was still convinced that justice would eventually be done. In early 1925, he made contact with a man he knew to be an ally from the past, Sir Arthur Conan Doyle, and begged him to try again on his behalf.

Conan Doyle approached the Secretary of State for Scotland and asked him to consider the case as Oscar Slater had already served more than fifteen years, the usual length of a life sentence at that time.

Sir Herbert Stephen, a prominent figure in English legal circles, took up arms on behalf of Slater as well, publishing an article decrying the manner in which Slater had been convicted and stating, most provocatively, that such a thing would never have happened in England.

John Trench was by now dead. He had died in 1919, age fifty, but his influence on the Slater case had not died with him. Trench had told a journalist friend the whole story before he left for foreign fields. The journalist was a man called William Park. In 1927, Park published a book, entitled *The Truth About Oscar Slater*, that was to cause a sensation. The book contained every single detail supplied to him by Trench, including Trench's theory about what had really happened on the night of Miss Gilchrist's death.

All hell broke loose. The newspapers were full of it. The Scottish legal system was held up to mockery. Statements supposedly from Nellie Lambie and Mary Barrowman were published in the press. Public pressure mounted. Oscar Slater should be released.

Gradually the pressure forced Sir John Gilmour, the Secretary of State for Scotland, to cave in. Oscar Slater was released from prison on 14 November 1927, after eighteen-and-a-half years in prison.

His supporters had not finished yet. Led by the indomitable Conan Doyle, they pressed for an inquiry into the case. Sir John Gilmour knew he had no choice but to agree. On 8 June 1928, the appeal began at the High Court in Edinburgh.

Slater was represented by Craigie Aitchison KC, who had done an admirable job in the past twelve months, gathering piles of evidence from witnesses and studying the statements and evidence that had been brought to court in 1909. Oscar himself was not to be called as a witness, and this caused him considerable anxiety. The last time this happened, things had gone very much against him. But his defence counsel was adamant.

Mr Craigie Aitchison was quite brilliant and very thorough. He punched holes in the Lord Advocate's case for the prosecution against Oscar Slater with consummate ease. He also condemned, quite unequivocally, the manner in which the character of Slater had been assassinated by the prosecution. This had undoubtedly biased his client's case. Finally, he was very critical of the conduct of Lord Guthrie, the judge in the Slater trial. In his final address, Lord Guthrie had denied Oscar Slater 'the full benefit of the presumption of innocence'.

Slater's conviction was quashed.

The story does have a happy ending, but the beginning was tragic and the middle should never be forgotten. It was a catalogue of catastrophic misdirection and prejudiced investigation. Oscar Slater was innocent, but while he languished in jail for nearly twenty years, somewhere a killer walked free.

THE DALKEITH POISONER

At Bridgend, tucked in a corner just on the edge of the old town of Dalkeith, stands The Neuk, an attractive house that was, around the turn of the twentieth century, the home of the Hutchison family. The owner of the house was Charles Hutchison, a Freemason and respected member of the community who worked for the Duke of Buccleuch. His son John was a more flamboyant figure, the proud owner of a flashy new car, who lived life recklessly, speculating in stocks and shares, womanising and enjoying the good life.

On 3 February 1911, the Hutchison family were having a celebration to mark the silver wedding anniversary of Charles and his wife. Eighteen people in total had assembled at the Hutchisons' home for the occasion; among them were Alfred Corrie and his wife and daughter from Musselburgh. John Hutchison was engaged to be married to Corrie's daughter.

The party was going well. The guests enjoyed some card games and a good supper. It was after midnight when the ladies retired to the drawing room, leaving the men to their whisky and cigars. After a short time, John brought coffee to the guests. Mrs Hutchison poured the coffee out for the ladies and they sat back to take a sip. At the first mouthful, one of the ladies noticed a strange and unpleasant taste. Unfortunately, her exclamation of surprise and warning to the others was too late, for all the others, except one, had already taken mouthfuls of the strange brew. The effects were swift and very painful. The ladies felt a terrible dryness in their throats and an accompanying severe abdominal pain. They began to retch and vomit uncontrollably. The men downstairs were suffering equally, if not more. As luck would have it, both Charles Hutchison and his friend, Alec Clapperton, a grocer from Musselburgh, had drunk the entire contents of their coffee cups in one go. A toast had been proposed and they had responded, not with whisky but with the coffee that they held in their hands at the time.

The scene became one of total chaos. Some guests, having rushed outside, either to seek some benefit from the fresh air or simply to be sick, collapsed and lay on the grass in front of the house, convulsed and moaning with pain. Only three of the guests remained well, having left their coffee untouched. It must have presented a most alarming picture to anyone passing by.

John Hutchison was very solicitous to the sick people, to such an extent that he even offered a mustard and water emetic to some of them. While John ministered to the stricken guests, one of the unaffected few went to get medical help.

Two doctors came to the house – Dr Mitchell and Dr Blackstock. When they examined the sick people, they immediately suspected that there had been some sort of poisoning, and they sent for the services of Dr Lovell Gulland from Edinburgh, who was an expert in such matters. In spite of the efforts of the three men, however, Charles Hutchison and Alec Clapperton died only a few hours later. The house next door, owned by a headmaster, Mr Sherrin, was commandeered for the sick people. Some of the sick were sufficiently recovered to return home later in the day, but others remained poorly for quite some time. Worst affected were Charles Hutchison's wife and Alec Clapperton's sister, Mary. The story was big news in the area, and before long cards, flowers and messages of sympathy were pouring in.

Over the next few days an investigation was set in motion to find the cause of the poisoning. The coffee had been made in an unusual tall, copper pot. Suspicion fell upon this as being the source of the trouble, but tests proved it to be harmless. John and his younger brother, Herbert, gave their full co-operation to the investigation but could not enlighten the police any further.

On 7 February the funeral of Charles Hutchison took place. It was well attended, with members of the Masons paying their respects at the graveside. Mrs Hutchison was too ill to attend her husband's funeral but John, the chief mourner, seemed to be overcome by emotion. He was very pale as he joined the gathering of mourners and he was seen to sway with apparent grief at his father's grave.

Alec Clapperton's funeral was a big affair, attended by some five hundred people. Many businesses in Musselburgh closed as a mark of respect on the day of the funeral. His death had sent shockwaves through the community.

The police investigation continued. Various items were removed from the house at Dalkeith. It was now evident that the poison that had affected the dinner-party guests had been arsenic, but where had it come from? Both Charles Hutchison's sons denied knowledge of any such substance having been in the house. Rumours, fuelled by press speculation, began to fly.

Inspector Forbes, the man who had been placed at the head of the inquiry, turned his attentions to chemists' shops in the area, in particular the shop where John Hutchison had been employed as an assistant dispenser. Careful records were kept of all the drugs that were stored in the shop, and a stock check supervised by the police soon revealed that a bottle of arsenic was missing. At once a warrant was issued for the arrest of John Hutchison.

Hutchison had seen this coming. Telling acquaintances that he was going to Newcastle for a day or so, he had taken off. His trail led to London. It was discovered that he had stayed there for one night, in a hotel close to the Strand. Detective Inspector John Laing, who was familiar with the suspect, followed the trail from London to the Channel Islands. Descriptions published in the newspapers proved to be very useful in helping the police to follow Hutchison as he moved from place to place. In spite of adopting false names, he was identified by someone wherever he went. Hutchison had gone to Jersey and then to Guernsey. On his arrival in Guernsey, a fellow-traveller had seen him buy a newspaper and quickly walk off, apparently in some distress. Another man had witnessed this and then, reading the paper himself, had recognised the description of Hutchison and contacted the police in London.

Police Sergeant Burley of Scotland Yard arrived in Guernsey on Monday 20 February and began a search of the boarding houses. His first call was fruitless, but when he went to the next house he found he was in luck. The owner of the establishment had already realised that a man who had registered there as a guest fitted the description of John Hutchison perfectly. He was in the parlour at that very moment.

Burley went into the parlour and confronted the man. The man claimed that the policeman must be mistaken. His name was not Hutchison, he said, but Henderson. He could prove it, he said. Sergeant Burley stood his ground and asked the man to accompany him. Hutchison, for Hutchison it was, followed the policeman to the door, as if he was going to co-operate. At the last moment, however, he broke free and rushed towards the stairs, fumbling in his pocket as he went. The policeman then saw him draw a phial of liquid from his pocket and put it to his lips. He tried to grab the phial and succeeded in knocking it from Hutchison's hand but not before Hutchison had swallowed some of the liquid. Burley watched in horror as Hutchison collapsed there and then. Within minutes he was dead. The phial that he had taken from his pocket had contained prussic acid – a lethal poison. The phial, if full, would probably have held enough to kill fifteen or sixteen people. Thus John Hutchison had spared himself the torment of facing the consequences of his terrible crime. His father and Alec Clapperton, his victims, had suffered for hours before they died, but John Hutchison ensured that his own suffering would not be prolonged. It was a cowardly escape after a brutal act.

Hutchison was buried on Guernsey, in St Peter's Port. His father's funeral might have been well attended, but John's was a bleak and lonely affair. No one mourned. The only people who saw John Hutchison go to his grave were those in a crowd of a hundred or so who had read about the poisonings and had come to stare as the coffin was carried to the graveyard.

What had motivated a young man of twenty-four years of age to commit such a callous and brutal act? Revelations about the life of John Hutchison after his death threw some light on the subject.

He was a young man sliding rapidly out of control. His family was already beginning to count the cost of John's reckless living. He had stolen from the family on one occasion, taking money from his father's safe while his parents were attending the local church. He might have been engaged to be married, but he had not confined his attentions to one girl only. He had, in fact, made another girl pregnant.

In addition to this, John Hutchison was in big money trouble. He had begun to speculate in stocks and shares some time before and, encouraged by a modest degree of success initially, had taken to gambling very rashly on the stock market with large sums of money. He had suffered terrible losses and, as a consequence, was deep in debt – to the tune of some £10,000. His father's life was well in-sured. If his parents died, then Hutchison would profit from their deaths by £4,000 in insurance money alone. He would also, no doubt, fall heir to his father's estate. This goes some way to finding a possible explanation for what Hutchison did. He was motivated by money – he needed it and saw how he could get it.

But what about the other guests at the party? Why did Hutchison poison them? There is one possible reason why he might have sought to get rid of one of the guests. One of the people to whom he owed money – more than a thousand pounds – was Alfred Corrie, his prospective father-in-law. It would certainly benefit Hutchison to be free of him. Perhaps this was why Hutchison had carefully arranged the date of the party at his father's house to ensure that Corrie and his family could attend – a case of trying to kill two birds with one stone.

Nevertheless, it seems a truly desperate act to try to kill eighteen people in one go. There must be some doubt as to whether or not Hutchison was sane when he carried out the deed. Did he think that he could get away with it? Was there some elaborate plan by which he might have hoped to escape retribution? We will never know. Hutchison took any explanation for his dreadful actions with him to the grave.

DEATH IN
BROUGHTY FERRY

On 3 November 1912 police broke into the home of Miss Jean Milne, Elmgrove House in Broughty Ferry, and found her fully clothed body lying at the foot of the stairs in the hall. She had not fallen. There were signs of a violent struggle having taken place, with bloodstains down the stairs and on the banisters, and splashes of blood on the walls and the floor. Miss Milne had been killed by several blows to her head, and the poker that had been used to kill her was lying, broken at its handle, close to her body on the hall floor. Miss Milne's feet had been tied together at the ankles with curtain cord. The telephone wire had been cut with garden shears, which had been left carelessly lying nearby, and, presumably in an attempt to avoid the early discovery of the body by an inquisitive postman or tradesman peering through a door or window, Miss Milne's battered corpse had been partially covered with sheeting and a curtain had been tied over the glass in the front door.

Jean Milne was sixty-five years old. She lived quite alone, by choice it would seem, for she had more than enough money to employ a live-in housekeeper and other domestic help as well. Elmgrove House, where she lived, was very large, but she kept herself confined to only a few rooms – a living room, kitchen, bedroom and bathroom. The other rooms in the house (of which there were at least ten) were kept permanently closed, their doors and windows securely sealed. Miss Milne had a reputation as a bit of a recluse, but in fairness she had done little to earn it. She did have friends, both men and women, and she had not withdrawn herself from society at all. She enjoyed shopping and spent occasional holidays in London or in the north of Scotland when the fancy took her. She was a regular attender at church on a Sunday. Her style of living was perhaps a little eccentric, but her house was, after all, her castle. How she lived there was very much her own business. She had lived alone since the death of her brother, who had shared the Broughty Ferry house with her. He had been a tobacco manufacturer in Dundee, a man of some wealth, and when he died Miss Milne had been left the house and a generous income for the time of around £1,000 per annum.

At once, we might begin to suspect that robbery was the primary motive for this terrible crime. Miss Milne was a wealthy woman, past her fittest at the age of sixty-five, and living on her own. She was an obvious target. Her body, although covered in the marks inflicted by the poker, had not received any one blow that could be considered a fatal wound. She had died from the trauma of the attack rather than from the wounds she had received. Her attacker had probably left her alive; perhaps he had wanted to silence her rather than kill her.

But if robbery was the motive, why were Miss Milne's fingers still adorned with their rings? Why did it appear that nothing had been taken from the house?

Miss Milne might well have known her killer. In the room that she used as both living and dining room, the table had been carefully set for high tea for two. The meat pie in the centre of the table was untouched and the china and cutlery had not been used. Who had Miss Milne been expecting to entertain?

There was no sign of a break-in – another indication that the victim had known her killer and let him or her into the house. The only thing that had alerted the attention of the police to Elmgrove House had been the fact that the postman had noticed the post-box filling up to the point of overflowing. It was not like Miss Milne to let such a thing happen. Even when she took a holiday, she made arrangements for her post to be dealt with.

A post-mortem examination was carried out, and it was announced that Miss Milne had probably lain dead for almost three weeks. The earliest postmark on the letters in her post-box was 14 October. Miss Milne had been seen alive on 15 October but on 16 October a church elder visiting the house had been unable to get an answer. In all probability, Miss Milne had died some time between 15 October and the time of the elder's visit.

There was just one problem with this theory. Another person, Alexander Troup, who had been employed as a gardener at Elmgrove House when Miss Milne's brother was alive, called at the house on 21 October to collect money for charity. According to him, although no one came to answer the door, he saw the figure of Miss Milne at an upstairs bedroom window, partially obscured by a curtain. Coming to the conclusion that he had called at an inconvenient time, he left and returned later. The first time he called, the cover had been over the lock on the front door, but when he called back later, again without getting any reply, he found the cover on the lock was up, revealing the keyhole. It appeared as if someone had used a key in the door. He knocked again at the door, but there was still no reply.

The police were baffled. If the woman at the window had been Miss Milne, then why had she not picked up her mail for the past few days and why had she not come to the door when Troup called? She knew the man and had always been quite willing to give money to charitable causes in the past. The post-mortem results suggested that the figure at the window that Troup had seen could not have been Miss Milne, for she would have been already dead. So who was it? Had there even been a figure at the window? And who had moved the cover on the front door lock that day?

The police believed now that the killer might have been a woman.

The blows that Miss Milne had received, although numerous, had not been as heavy as might have been expected. No single one had been inflicted with enough force to kill her. And Troup had seen a woman at the window upstairs. Of course he would assume that the woman was Miss Milne, so he might not have looked as carefully as he might have done. In other words, he 'saw' the person whom he expected to see.

Detective-Lieutenant John Thomson Trench of the Glasgow police was a man with a considerable reputation. He was called in to take over the murder inquiry and arrived in Dundee on Monday 4 November. He carried out a careful examination of the scene of the crime. He found a cigar butt among the ashes in the grate in the living-room fireplace. Miss Milne had kept company with a man at her home in the recent past. She was in the habit of using the living-room fire – the absence of smoke from the chimney was one of the things that the neighbours had noticed in the days leading up to the discovery of her body. Could the cigar butt constitute significant evidence?

John Trench also took note of something else, something that had been dismissed by the Dundee police as being insignificant. A two-pronged carving fork had been found in the hall, tucked underneath a chest. Trench had a closer look at it, for it had certainly been out of place. It belonged, by rights, in the dining area, beside the knife that came with it in the carving set.

Trench then examined Miss Milne's clothes, which had been kept as evidence, and found something that had not been noticed by anyone else. There were holes in the clothing consistent with the two-pronged fork having been stuck through with some force. Trench wanted to examine the body of Miss Milne. Surely it would bear the marks of wounds inflicted by the carving fork. But Miss Milne was already underground by this time – she had been buried on 5 November – and Trench was unable to get permission for an exhumation of the body. If Trench's assumptions were correct and

127

Miss Milne had been stabbed by the carving fork, then it was quite surprising that the marks that would have been left on her body by such an instrument had been overlooked in the post-mortem examination.

Trench was convinced by this time that the killer had been a man. The police now had to trawl through the statements of various witnesses and friends of Miss Milne to try to establish the identity of any possible suspects. In order to give their inquiries added momentum, the police offered a reward of £100 to anyone who could come forward with information that would lead to a conviction. It certainly helped to set the tongues a-wagging. Witnesses began to appear down at the police station.

The police discovered that there was a man with whom Miss Milne had struck up a friendship in the recent past. Miss Milne had confided in two of her women friends that she had met someone. Her friends were quite intrigued, for Miss Milne's manner when she spoke of this man was uncharacteristically girlish. She seemed to be quite smitten. The man was considerably younger than Miss Milne, it was said. He was probably little more than forty. Miss Milne had spoken to John Wood, a man who visited Elmgrove House from time to time to attend to the garden, and had told him that she had met a German gentleman during a recent four-month visit to London. Not long after that, John had the opportunity of seeing for himself a man whom he presumed to be the gentleman in question. On 19 September he had been working at Elmgrove House and was just about to leave when the man had arrived at the house; it was about 5.30 p.m. Miss Milne had greeted her visitor with great enthusiasm. She was obviously quite thrilled that he had come to see her. The man was fair and well built – stoutish, in fact – and he had a moustache. He had a cheery face and wore a tweed hat. He appeared to be quite a gentleman and spoke with an accent. John Wood, having heard about Miss Milne's German friend, naturally took the visitor's accent to be German.

Just after this visit, Miss Milne had left Brought Ferry for a tour of the Highlands. A witness who saw her on her return journey on a steamer in the Caledonian Canal noticed that she seemed to be in the company of a tall man.

It looked as if the man in question had kept up his friendship with Miss Milne during October. There were quite a few witnesses to this.

A maid in a neighbouring house had seen a tall, handsome man walking in her garden one morning in October. The man had paced up and down in a preoccupied manner. His appearance had been somewhat incongruous, for it was mid-morning and he was dressed in evening clothes.

Miss Milne had visited the local wine merchant on a shopping trip in October and had indicated that she was expecting company – a man. She had been most insistent about the quality of whisky and wine she was purchasing.

Neighbours had noticed a man hanging around the Milne house.

A local taxi driver had given a fair, moustached man with an accent a lift from Dundee, dropping him off as requested close to Elmgrove House, on 15 October. The taxi driver thought that the man's accent was an English one. The man had seemed to be rather agitated. The taxi driver claimed that he had been 'sinister' – this claim was made, remember, after it had become known that a murderer was being sought by the police.

Finally, a dustman on his rounds in the district on 16 October had noticed a man, about thirty years old, thin and pale, wearing a bowler hat, emerging from the gate at Elmgrove House. The man had ducked behind the gate when he realised the presence of the dustman in the street and had emerged only after the dustman had moved on past the house.

Interestingly, none of the descriptions of the man that the various witnesses claimed to have seen quite matched up. A tall man, a man of about five foot nine inches – hardly similar. Well built or thin? A German accent or an English accent – which was it?

From German, to English, to American . . . the change in direction of the police inquiry was quite dramatic and, in retrospect, a little bizarre. Charles Warner was an impecunious Canadian, in fact. There was evidence to suggest that Miss Milne had met a 'dashing American' while she was staying in London on her last trip. The police took this line of inquiry one step further – it was to be a step in the wrong direction – and Warner had the misfortune of being in the wrong place at the wrong time. When the police in Scotland contacted Scotland Yard for their assistance in finding the American with whom Miss Milne had become acquainted, Warner was in police custody in Kent for the non-payment of a restaurant bill. Witnesses in London (the Strand Palace Hotel and the Bonnington Hotel) were not quite so sure, but the good people of Broughty Ferry were surprisingly willing to overlook the differences between their previous descriptions of the stranger around Elmgrove House and the actual appearance of Warner in the photographs that they were shown. He was fair and he was foreign. He would do.

John Trench travelled to England to arrest Warner as he came out of police custody. Warner was strenuously protesting his innocence. Trench was himself far from convinced that this was the right man. The witnesses had very possibly been more consumed with the thrill of helping to catch a murderer (and thus profiting from the reward) than with making sure that this was the man whom they had seen with Miss Milne or around her house. By the time the journey from England was over, Trench was sure that Charles Warner was an innocent man.

Warner and Trench arrived in Dundee and Warner appeared before the sheriff to be formally charged with the murder of Jean Milne. Trench, meanwhile, wasted no time in acting upon the information that Warner had given him in the course of their long journey from London. He left for Antwerp at once.

Warner claimed to have arrived in London on 18 October. Prior to that date and, most importantly, on the date of Miss Milne's death, he had been in Antwerp. For a panicky moment or two, Warner had been unable to think of any means by which he could prove this fact. He had been sleeping rough, so no hotel would have a record of his having stayed in the city. He had been travelling alone, so he had no friends to testify to his presence in Antwerp at the crucial time. Then he remembered the one thing that could save him, with Trench's help. He had pawned a waistcoat in Antwerp on 16 October. He still had the ticket.

Trench's mission was not an easy one, for the journey was long and he had to find his way to a small shop in an obscure part of a foreign city he had not been to before. But Warner had given him some directions and Trench's detective's nose did not let him down. He found the pawn shop, checked the ticket against the date in the owner's records, and retrieved the waistcoat. It was not long before he was on the boat back to Britain with the evidence he needed to prevent a wrongful conviction.

In one respect Trench had failed. The murderer of Jean Milne was never found. After the furore surrounding the arrest and subsequent release of Charles Warner, the investigation lost momentum and ground to a halt. But there was still reason to celebrate. Trench had succeeded in preventing a major miscarriage of justice. Of that he could certainly be proud. It was perhaps this success that moved him to take up the case of Oscar Slater, who was languishing in jail for a crime that Trench – and many others – believed he had not committed. His work on behalf of Oscar Slater would cost him his career, but for now, with Charles Warner effusive in his gratitude to him, Trench could feel that the pursuit of justice was a worthwhile cause.

PATRICK HIGGINS

Patrick Higgins was a labourer, thought to be of relatively low intelligence and definitely of little means. He worked hard and he drank hard. His work took him travelling around West Lothian touting for jobs. He was married and had two young sons, named John and William. His wife cared for the children while her husband struggled to make a living, but while the two boys were still very young, she died, and Patrick was left to manage on his own.

There can be no doubt that he found it very hard. The constant search for work and money was difficult enough without the added burden of small boys to care for. He did not cope with them very well at all and soon found himself in trouble for neglecting them. For a while, the boys were placed in care with a family in West Lothian, but they were soon returned to their father when he failed to keep up with payments for their care.

It was clear to those who knew him that Higgins did not really care for the boys and found them to be a considerable burden. Nonetheless, the boys remained with their father for a while. It was in November 1911 that people noticed that the boys had gone. Higgins told those who asked that he had met two women on a train who had taken a strong liking to his sons. The women were quite well-to-do, Higgins said, and had no children of their own to look after. It had seemed like the perfect solution. The boys could have a comfortable life in a good home. Higgins had handed over his sons there and then. The break was to be a complete one, apparently. Higgins would have no more contact with the children. He did not even know where the boys were being taken. It was all for the best.

This story must have seemed very strange to those who heard it, and, undoubtedly, people must have been suspicious. The boys had clearly been a burden to Higgins since his wife's death. In addition, he had already been found guilty of neglecting John and William. Nonetheless, there was nothing concrete to suggest that Higgins was lying when he told of the boys' 'adoption'.

If he grieved for the loss of his sons, Higgins certainly did not show it. He carried on much as he had done before. In bad weather, or when he had enough money, he sometimes stayed in bed and breakfast establishments, but he camped out in the open air for much of the time, close to wherever he was working. He cooked basic meals on his shovel over an open fire. For pleasure, he generally resorted to large quantities of drink.

The subject of Patrick Higgins' children remained closed for well over a year. Then in 1913, as midsummer was approaching, two ploughmen working near a disused quarry on Niddry Mains farm made a grisly discovery. They noticed something large floating in the murky waters of a quarry. On closer inspection, they were horrified to realise that the object had a distinctly human form. They set to work to drag the thing towards the edge of the water and immediately realised that what they had come across were the bodies of two small boys, bound together with rope.

The bodies had been remarkably well preserved, but forensic examination revealed that they had been in the water for a long time – somewhere between eighteen months and two years.

The police did quite a remarkable job in their investigations. Not only were they able to discover the identity of the two dead boys (they were John and William, the two sons of Patrick Higgins), but they were also able to trace the last person who had seen them alive in November 1911 – a woman who had fed them some hot soup.

Patrick Higgins was arrested and charged with the murder of his sons. He was sent to Calton Prison pending trial. The trial took place in September 1913.

Throughout the process, it was noted that Higgins showed little emotion, if any at all. Nor was there any sign that he felt remorse for what he had done. Whilst it was accepted that he had killed his sons, his defence claimed that he was not guilty of murder as he had been insane at the time. There was some evidence, backed up with medical opinion, that Higgins might be an epileptic. The defence team claimed that because of his epilepsy Higgins had not been in his right mind at the time of the killings.

Higgins was thoroughly examined by doctors and pronounced mentally fit. What had been taken to be episodes of fitting were most likely to have been alcohol induced. The claim that he was insane could not stand.

The jury found Patrick Higgins guilty of the double murder, and the judge duly sentenced him to death. Higgins reacted to the pronouncement with the same flatness of mood that he had displayed throughout. There was little sympathy for him.

Executions were no longer public. The hanging of Eugene Marie Chantrelle had been the first private execution in Edinburgh, and the public had shown some disappointment at not getting a glimpse of the grisly spectacle. It seemed as if they felt the same when Higgins was due to hang on 2 October 1913. A silent crowd gathered on Calton Hill as the hour of execution drew closer. At a few minutes past eight in the morning, a black flag was raised above the jail for the assembled people to see. Patrick Higgins was dead.

JOHN DONALD
MERRET

John Donald Merret came from a broken home, but all the same his background was hardly deprived. An only child, he was born in 1908 in Southport in Cheshire. The family then travelled to Russia, where Mr Merret, an engineer, had been offered a lucrative job. Mrs Bertha Merret and her son did not stay in Russia for long. Mrs Merret took young Donald off to Switzerland, a country she liked much better, and there they stayed. World War I broke out in 1914 and during the war years, Mr and Mrs Merret lost touch. It does not appear that either of them was sorry. They never saw each other again.

During the war, things began to get a little too hot in Europe for Bertha Merret's liking. She was quite a wealthy woman in her own right and could well afford another move overseas. She chose New Zealand, where Donald spent most of his schooldays. In 1924, when Donald was sixteen, mother and son came back to Great Britain, and Donald was enrolled in the prestigious Malvern College to finish off his schooling.

Mrs Merret had high hopes for her son: he was a bright lad and she could afford the best of education. She wanted him to attend university and, after considering various possibilities, finally settled for Edinburgh. Edinburgh had a fine university, and it was also the sort of place where she could be happy. Donald could stay with her (she liked to keep a close eye on her beloved son), attending his university classes during the day and returning to his dear mama every evening. The Merrets rented a flat in Buckingham Terrace, a very respectable address in the west end of the city, and they moved in.

It seemed as if everything was sailing along very smoothly. Donald breakfasted with his mother every day, set off to classes and returned home in the evening when, after a meal with his mother, he retired to his room to study before turning in for the night. The bedroom door was always locked securely. Donald said that he wanted to avoid interruption (by whom?) and, what was more, he said, he felt safer in a locked room for he had found himself sleepwalking of late and waking up in the strangest of places.

All was not as it seemed, however. Donald was living a secret and very full double life. To be fair, he had started off quite well and had attended classes at the university for a few weeks, but his enthusiasm had rapidly waned when he found there were far better ways to spend one's time in the capital city. Wine, women and song were now Donald Merret's subjects of choice. Every night, while his mother fondly imagined him burning the midnight oil with his nose buried in the depths of some hefty tome (he might be working too hard, he seemed so dreadfully tired!), Donald was out on the town.

He was quite ingenious in his efforts to keep his nocturnal activities a secret. Donald's room was at the front of the house, while his mother's was at the back. Donald's room, quite conveniently, had a balcony overlooking the street. His 'sleepwalking' had been such a worry to his mother that she had tied a rope across the balcony to prevent her somnambulant son from toppling to disaster. Her son, very much awake, used the rope to make his descent into the street below (and his return the following morning) just that little bit more convenient.

Donald's favourite place of entertainment was the Dunedin Palais de Danse, which was in Picardy Place in the east end of the centre of town. Day or night, Donald could find plenty to occupy his time here. He made the acquaintance of two employees there, to whom he became particularly attached. One was Betty Christie, the other was George Scott. Both were 'dancing partners' at the palais, whose services could be employed, either in or out of the dance hall, for a certain fee. They had a tremendous time together, the three of them. Donald bought himself a motorbike, then another complete with sidecar. Their outings became more adventurous and all the more enjoyable.

Of course, the high life was expensive. Donald had a reasonable weekly allowance from his mother, who liked to keep track of everything he spent. But he could never have afforded the company of his two new friends on what his mother gave him every week. Luckily for Donald, his mother did not keep quite such a close eye on what she (officially) spent. Mrs Merret had a current account with the Clydesdale Bank, which she used for her everyday needs. Obviously, she saw no need to check her balance regularly, for she had ensured that there was a generous 'float'. Donald, in a most enterprising fashion, practised his mother's signature a few times until it looked just right, took himself off to the bank and cashed a cheque for himself. Then he cashed another, and another, and another.

Mrs Merret got a letter from the bank. Funds in her current account were dangerously low. Before long, she would be overdrawn. Could she please arrange for the immediate transfer of funds from her deposit account to avert this undesirable outcome?

Mrs Merret was quite disturbed when she got the letter. She turned her attention to her bank balance and the withdrawals that had been made. It was 16 March 1926.

The next day began much as normal. Henrietta Sutherland, the daily help, arrived at the house in time to clear away the breakfast things. She set to work, washing the dishes and tending to the fire. In the sitting room, Donald was relaxing in an armchair while his mother sat at her desk attending to business.

Suddenly Henrietta was stunned to hear a loud bang, followed by a loud thud, as if something, or someone heavy had fallen in the sitting room. Donald burst into the kitchen, shouting that his mother had shot herself. Henrietta ran through to the sitting room and found Mrs Merret lying on the floor with blood pouring from her ear. The police and ambulance were summoned, and Mrs Merret, who was miraculously still alive, was rushed to the Royal Infirmary of Edinburgh.

Donald had stated that his mother had shot herself. At that time suicide was a crime. Accordingly, Mrs Merret was placed in the locked ward reserved for cases such as hers. Whether or not this highly respectable lady was aware of the humiliation of it all, we do not know. During the time that she was in hospital, Donald found a nice hotel room for himself and Betty Christie and continued with his hedonistic lifestyle much as if nothing had happened. He visited his mother one or two times, but that was all. He had given his statement to the police and they had believed him. According to Donald, he had approached his mother to speak to her while she was working at her desk. She had told him to go away. He had turned his back on her and then he had heard a loud bang. He had wheeled round just in time to see his poor mother fall to the ground, bleeding.

The police had noticed the bank statements on Mrs Merret's desk. She was having financial difficulties. It seemed reasonable to suppose that she could not bear the shame of finding herself with debts building up. Donald Merret's story was entirely credible.

Mrs Merret recovered sufficiently to give her own version of events to doctors at the hospital. She told them that she had been sitting at her desk, writing, when Donald had approached and had stood beside her. She had said to him, 'Go away, Donald, and don't annoy me.' The next thing she had been aware of was a sudden loud bang. She had been aware of nothing else until she had woken up in hospital.

It is unlikely that the doctors believed what Mrs Merret told them. She contracted meningitis as a result of her injuries and died on 1 April. Donald made time to attend the funeral and then returned to the important business of enjoying himself. It must have seemed strange that an only child, so close to his mother, took so little time to mourn her passing. But Donald, freed from his mother's apron strings at last, not caring what other people might think, took himself off on a little holiday.

Mrs Merret's bankers remained interested in their dead client, however. The way in which Mrs Merret's finances had suddenly taken a turn for the worse was most uncharacteristic. Mrs Merret had always been such a reliable client. They turned their attentions to the cheques that had been cashed in the period leading up to her death. The signatures did not quite match up. The police were informed, and in November Donald Merret was arrested and charged with the murder of his mother and the forgery of cheques from her account, amounting to the sum of £457. The trial began in February at the High Court in Edinburgh.

Donald Merret sat silently in the dock as the trial got under way. Medical experts appointed by both sides began a lengthy debate as to whether or not Mrs Merret's death had been suicide.

The police had not done their job properly when they had been called to the Merret household after the shooting. Of that there can be little doubt. A woman lay dying from a bullet wound on the carpet. Her son stood at her side. Where was the gun? Whose fingerprints had been upon the weapon?

The gun had been on the desk, and one of the officers had picked it up. He had not thought, as we might, that if Mrs Merret had shot herself the gun might have remained in her hand or at least fallen to the floor when she did rather than being replaced neatly on the desk. The weapon had never been dusted for fingerprints. No search had been carried out in the sitting room in Buckingham Terrace and much later, when Mr Penn, Mrs Merret's brother-in-law, had found a spent cartridge on the floor by a wall and had taken it to the police, they had paid little attention. On the morning of the shooting, the attending officers had asked Henrietta Sutherland and Donald Merret for their versions of events and that had more or less satisfied them. The doctors in the Royal Infirmary had heard Mrs Merret's side of the story, but the police had never taken a statement from her.

Henrietta Sutherland had in fact told the police two different stories. At first, she had said that she had been in the kitchen when she heard the shot. Then Donald had come in to tell her that his mother had shot herself. Later, her story had changed somewhat and she had claimed that she had heard the shot, rushed into the sitting room and seen Mrs Merret, holding the gun, falling to the floor. In court, she went back to her first story. She admitted to the court that she had been rather carried away with the excitement of it all when she had given her second account to the police. Donald's defence counsel, Craigie Aitchison, did his best, but she would not be persuaded otherwise. No, she had not seen Mrs Merret fall.

The forensic scientists then put forward their cases. Could the wound in Mrs Merret's ear have been caused by a shot from her own hand or had she been shot from farther away? There were arguments for both sides. Mrs Merret's ear was produced in evidence. Where were the powder burns that were consistent with shooting at close range? Could they have been washed away by the blood? Neither side could prove beyond doubt that their theory was correct.

The forgery charge was easier to prove, and there was little doubt that Donald had been stealing money from his mother. He was found guilty of this charge by a unanimous verdict, but on the charge of murder, ten out of the fifteen jurors found the case not proven while five found him not guilty. Merret was sentenced to twelve months in prison – a mere hiccup in his villainous career.

Upon his release from prison in 1928, John Donald Merret took himself off to England, where he availed himself of the hospitality offered by one of his mother's friends, Mrs Bonnar, from Hastings. He also availed himself of her seventeen-year-old daughter, Isobel Veronica Bonnar (known as 'Vera'), and ran back to Scotland with her, where they were married. In honour of the occasion, Donald gave himself a new name: Ronald Chesney. Donald had been left quite a respectable sum of money from his mother's estate, but that evaporated rapidly. Unperturbed, Donald kept his cheque book handy and travelled the country with Vera, writing rubber cheques that were still bouncing when he was miles away. The police in the north of England finally caught up with him in Newcastle. Ronald Chesney was given a six-month sentence for his sins and Vera returned to her mother in Hastings to wait patiently for his release.

Donald, alias Ronald, was soon back on the pleasure trail. He came of age in 1929 and inherited a very large sum of money from his grandfather's estate. £50,000 richer, he bought himself a large house in Hastings and employed a retinue of servants. He bought a yacht, and once he had mastered the art of sailing, realised the full potential of this exciting new sport by taking up smuggling. He moved from Hastings to Surrey, buying a large house in Weybridge. Life became very hectic with wild parties at home and wild adventures on the open seas. In his spare time, Ronald indulged in a spot of blackmail as well.

Big houses, gambling and general extravagance cost him dearly, in spite of his lucrative smuggling activities. He expanded the smuggling enterprise, buying a larger boat and taking the family with him on an extended 'holiday'. His mother-in-law came too, although neither she nor Vera knew that the holiday was a cover for drugs and arms smuggling. They sailed round the Mediterranean, stopping off here and there, partying in every port, until Ronald's dwindling assets and mounting debts forced them to beat a hasty retreat back to England.

Vera and her mother realised that they would have to do something to bring in some money. To this end, they bought a large house in Ealing on their return to Britain and turned it into a guest house for elderly people. Life in Ealing must have seemed rather dull to Ronald Chesney after all his adventures on the high seas. But he was not to be grounded for long. World War II was about to break out. Ronald joined the Royal Navy.

Ronald's naval career was as colourful as the rest of his life. He was rapidly promoted to lieutenant. He revelled in the excitement and soon earned himself a reputation as a daredevil and eccentric. He managed to fit in the odd smuggling expedition here and there. He was captured and imprisoned in Italy but faked illness and got himself repatriated. Before long, he was back in action, promoted to lieutenant-commander. When the war ended, he was sent to Germany to assist in the allied operations there. Germany was full of opportunities for a man like Chesney. The black market offered the perfect chance to make a bit of money on the side.

Germany offered a romantic interest as well. Vera was far away in Ealing, and she and Ronald had become quite disenchanted with each other some time before. Ronald had always had an eye for a pretty girl, and he soon found a new partner to share his life in Germany. Her name was Gerda Schaller. For the next few years, Ronald spent most of his time with Gerda, travelling back to Britain rarely. He pressed Vera for a divorce, but she would have none of it. His life with Gerda was punctuated by short spells of imprisonment. He was sentenced to four months by the Royal Navy for stealing a car, he spent two months in prison in France on a smuggling charge and then a further four months, also in France, for forging a passport for Gerda. Finally, on a trip back to England in 1949 he was sent to prison for smuggling; this time the contraband was nylon stockings, a precious commodity in the post-war years.

In 1950, Chesney returned to Germany and took up with

another girlfriend. Once again he was desperately short of money. He tried his hand at smuggling again, and it was not long before he earned himself another twelve months in prison. When he was released, he redoubled his efforts to improve his financial situation. His enterprising skills came into play one last time.

Several years before, when Chesney still had some of the money that his grandfather had left him, he had generously set up a trust fund for Vera, worth £8,400. Vera was to earn the interest on it, but should she die, Merret stood to inherit the lot. There was no doubt in Chesney's mind that Vera had to go. The question was how? It took Chesney a while to draw up his plan.

It should have worked out beautifully. Vera was a heavy drinker, virtually an alcoholic. A simple drowning accident would do the trick. In order to cover his tracks, Chesney made himself a forged passport and used it when he entered Britain. He then arrived at the guest house in Ealing on Wednesday 10 February 1954 and declared his wish for a reconciliation with Vera. He got her exceedingly drunk with remarkable ease and then, exactly as he had planned, he drowned her in the bath.

Chesney's plan had not taken account of his mother-in-law's presence in the house, however. No sooner had he extinguished the life of his inebriated spouse than he was confronted with the vision of Mrs Bonnar coming along the hall with a tray of coffee. Chesney panicked, grabbed the coffee pot and beat his mother-in-law senseless with it, finishing the job by strangling her.

By the time the elderly residents in the Ealing guest house found the bodies of Mrs Bonnar and Mrs Chesney the next day, their killer was far from the scene, on his way back to Germany. But it did not take the police long to work out who was the most obvious suspect. Ronald was Donald and he had to be the killer. A full-scale hunt was on to find him.

The villain's brass neck was astonishing. From Cologne, where he thought he was safe, he wrote to his solicitors expressing his regret to hear that his wife had died and reminding them that he was now entitled to the sum of £8,400. How long did it take him to realise that he had given the police a lead on his trail? Not very long. Merret, alias Chesney, knew that time was running out. What awaited him back in Britain was not another short spell in prison but a short rope with a noose at the end. This he could not bear. In one final act of bravado – or cowardice – he took himself off into the middle of some woodland near Cologne on 16 February 1954 and shot himself in the mouth. This time there was no doubt about the suicide verdict.

STANISLAV MYSZKA

Catherine MacIntyre lived with her husband Peter and their grown-up son Archie in Tower Cottage, an attractive whitewashed building on Tombuie Estate, between Kenmore and Aberfeldy in Perthshire. Catherine worked in the big house and Peter was a shepherd on the estate. Their cottage was in a quiet situation, nearly a mile from the main road. It was secluded but beautiful, and life was peaceful there.

Things took a terrible turn on 26 September 1947. Catherine did not turn up for her duties at the big house. This was quite out of character, and in the afternoon, when there was still no sign of her, another estate worker went to Tower Cottage to find out whether everything was all right. He found Catherine's son, Archie, outside the front door, also concerned because the house was locked and there was no sign of either of his parents.

The two men had no choice but to break into the house. There they found the body of Catherine in a downstairs bedroom. She had been bound and gagged with brutal force and battered to death.

The police in Perth were alerted by the local constabulary and swept into action at once. It was clear, however, that they were not going to catch the culprit as he made his getaway. He had had plenty of time to get well away from the scene of the crime. A quick search around Tower Cottage revealed that money, clothes and jewellery, including Catherine MacIntyre's wedding ring, had been taken. Robbery had obviously been the motive for the killing, but the theft had not amounted to all that much in value (approximately £80 was taken) and the amount of force used in killing Catherine was quite horrific – certainly out of all proportion to what the robber stood to gain. It was a sickening crime.

On post-mortem examination, it was found that Catherine had been killed in the second half of the morning. Four blows had been inflicted on her skull with tremendous violence. Police teams searching the surrounding area found the murder weapon a couple of days later. It was a sawn-off shotgun. The gun was covered in bloodstains and was broken. The stock of the shotgun had most likely been used to beat Catherine MacIntyre to death. Beside the gun, which was found in a hiding place in bushes less than half a mile from the cottage, were some overalls, a razor and a handkerchief. Lastly, police found a railway ticket, the date on it 25 September – the day before Catherine's death.

Police questioned anybody and everybody who might have seen something that might point them in the direction of the killer. One possible suspect came to light in the course of their investigations. A man with a foreign accent was reported to have jumped into a taxi in Aberfeldy on the day of the murder. He was travelling all the way to Perth. He had had a severe cough and his shoes were remarkable for the amount of mud that was caked on them. The man was believed to be Polish.

The hunt for the mysterious Pole spread farther afield as the investigation progressed. Police at first concentrated their inquiries locally, starting with Taymouth Castle, which was used as a centre to help to resettle former Polish soldiers after the war, but when their efforts drew a blank there, they turned their attentions nationwide. The railway ticket had been issued in Perth, but there was no reason to suppose that the murderer's journey had begun there. Appeals were put out in the press and on radio for anyone who could come forward to assist them with the investigation. A description of the Polish man whom police sought to question was issued, along with details of the sawn-off shotgun that had been used to silence Mrs MacIntyre with such deadly effect.

The tactic worked. A worker on an estate in Aberdeenshire came forward and told the police that the weapon might well be his. It did in fact turn out to belong to him. He told the investigating officers that he had lent it to a man who lived locally – a farm labourer – not very long before. The gun had then gone missing from the labourer's house. Significantly, the disappearance of the gun had coincided with the departure of another labourer on the same farm. This labourer had been Polish.

The police now had the identity of their prime suspect. His name was Stanislav Myszka. They could connect him to the murder weapon and also to the bloodstained handkerchief that had been found beside it. The handkerchief had been given to Myszka by the farm labourer's wife shortly before he left.

Surprisingly, the police did not have far to look to find out where Myszka had gone after the killing. A fellow Pole, who was employed on a farm in Buchan, came forward and told the police that Myszka had been staying with him for a few days and had then left, saying that he was going to Peterhead. The search was closing in. Eventually Stanislav Myszka was arrested at Longside, where he had been hiding out in an abandoned building at an old air force station. He was found in possession of several of the missing items from Tower Cottage, including Catherine MacIntyre's wedding ring.

Stanislav Myszka stood trial at Perth High Court in January 1948. Myszka tried, at first, to plead insanity owing to the stress of worrying about his future. He was in fact a deserter from the Polish army and he was consumed with anxiety about his family back in Poland. This tactic had to be dropped, however, when Myszka was examined by doctors and found to be quite fit to plead. His plea then changed to not guilty for the murder charge. He admitted the theft but claimed that he had not killed Catherine MacIntyre.

The evidence against him was strong, however. The police had found the gun that had been used as a battering weapon. Myszka had stolen the gun from the farm near Aberdeen. Myszka had also been the owner of the bloodstained handkerchief found beside the shotgun. Finally, forensic examination of hairs found on the razor, which had been lying beside the handkerchief and the gun, revealed that in all probability the razor had been used by Myszka.

The jury had no difficulty in reaching their decision. Myszka was found guilty as charged and, still a young man at the age of twenty-three, was sentenced to death for his crime. Sentence was carried out on 6 February 1948 in Perth Prison. Stanislav Myszka was the last person to suffer the death penalty in Perth and the tenth last to be executed in Scotland.

PETER MANUEL

The list of crimes committed by Peter Manuel spans a period of twenty years. He started offending in boyhood and he was still a relatively young man when he was finally executed. As time went on, the frequency and violence of his crimes escalated; had he not been stopped when he was, the potential cost in human life is unthinkable. His final spree of violence lasted less than two months; in that short time he killed five people. He appeared to be driven by evil.

His attitude to his crimes was hard to understand. On the one hand, he made efforts to avoid detection, but on the other hand a definite need for attention was manifest in his actions. Sometimes it seemed as if he wanted to be caught. Whether this was because he wanted to be stopped or because he wanted in some bizarre way to take credit for his crimes is not clear. What is clear is that Peter Manuel was not one of those killers who has a quiet and respectable facade and a secret 'other' life. He wanted to be known as a hard man. He worked hard to earn his reputation; he wanted respect for it.

Peter Thomas Anthony Manuel was hanged for multiple murder on Friday 11 July 1958. The catalogue of crimes of which he was found guilty was horrific. As well as several counts of burglary, Manuel was found guilty of the murder of eight people in total. During his trial for these crimes, he was also wanted for another murder, that of a taxi driver in Newcastle, called Sidney Dunn. When his trial was over, as he awaited execution in Glasgow's Barlinnie Prison, Peter Manuel confessed to the murder of three other people. Twelve deaths; were there more than this? That has to be a possibility. What is certain, however, is that if he had not been stopped, the tally of dead would have risen. Manuel was ruthless and seemed to need the sense of power that killing gave him.

Manuel's violent tendencies had begun to show themselves at an early age. He had been in trouble with the authorities for various things, spending time in borstal (the equivalent then of a young offenders' institution) on and off between the ages of eleven and eighteen, for housebreaking, violence and indecent assault. It was inevitable that he would end up in prison, and he was sent to Peterhead Prison for nine years when he was only eighteen.

Prison did not have the desired effect – he came out as bad as he went in.

In 1956, Peter Manuel committed the first of the offences for which he would be hanged. On 4 January, the body of a woman was found at the edge of a golf course in East Kilbride. She was seventeen-year-old Anne Kneilands. Her skull had been smashed with an iron bar. Her underclothes had been interfered with, but she had not been sexually assaulted.

The Lanarkshire constabulary launched a high-profile and wide-ranging investigation into the murder. One witness had heard sounds of screaming coming from the golf course on the night of the murder but had not taken any steps to investigate the matter. Apart from that, the police had little to go on. Anne had been going to meet a boy whom she had become acquainted with the week before, but he had stood her up and she had been heading for home. The conductress on the bus remembered her. But no one else had seen her after that.

Peter Manuel was questioned about the murder. He had a history of violent and sexual assaults against women. He had scratch marks on his face. Could the police find anything to connect him with the crime? A search was carried out at the home of Manuel's parents. Forensic tests were conducted on some of the suspect's clothing, but no evidence was found to link Manuel with the girl's death. The police remained suspicious but could prove nothing. Manuel was free to commit murder again.

He did not wait long. On 17 September, seventeen-year-old Vivienne Watt was found fatally injured and her mother, Marion, and her aunt, Mrs Margaret Brown, were found dead in the Watts' home in Fennsbank Avenue in Glasgow. The three victims were found in bed. They had all been shot. The cleaning woman who made the grisly discovery called the police and the ambulance, but Vivienne too was dead before the emergency services arrived.

Vivienne's father, William Watt, came under suspicion. He had been away from home at the time of the killings, supposedly on a fishing trip in Argyll. Could he have made the trip back to Glasgow during the night to kill the three women, then travelled back to his hotel in Lochgilphead in time for breakfast? It was possible.

William Watt was arrested for the murders and spent more than two months in prison before the charges against him were dropped. His eventual release was due, in fact, to the efforts of the real killer – a manifestation of his bizarre need for attention. He did not appear to like someone else getting the credit for his crimes.

Manuel had been questioned about the killings. He had publicly boasted of intending to commit such a crime. He had even told some people that he was in possession of a gun. But the police had been unable to pin anything on him. He was, however, awaiting trial for a burglary at Hamilton Colliery, and by the time Mr Watt was arrested and confined, Manuel was beginning a prison sentence. In prison, Manuel started to boast that he knew about the killings. He knew William Watt was innocent and could prove it.

He took matters further when he wrote to Watt's defence solicitor and said he had been told details of the killings that had not been released to the public. Watt's counsel visited Manuel and listened to what he had to say. Undeniably, Manuel knew things about the Watt killings that had not been made public knowledge.

He also said that the person who had killed the Watt women had committed another offence using the same gun not long before the Watt killings. He had broken into the home of the Platt family in Bothwell Bridge to burgle the premises; he had also shot holes in a mattress. Watt's counsel did not believe for one moment that Manuel's story about another individual having committed the crimes was true, but it was not his job to prove this. He told the police about it, and they carried out another unsuccessful search of Manuel's home. Armed with Manuel's story, the solicitor was able to secure Watt's release from prison in December 1956.

Manuel was still one step ahead of the police, in spite of the fact that his warped desire to keep attention focused on him brought him dangerously close to being caught. Police, press and public who were familiar with the case all thought that Manuel was guilty. They just could not prove it. It was as if Manuel was challenging the police to a game of 'catch me if you can'. When Manuel was released from prison in November 1957, there must have been dread in the hearts of the Scottish constabulary.

Manuel did not commit his next crime in Scotland, however. He was returning from Newcastle to Edinburgh in a taxi when he murdered again. The body of Sidney Dunn was found on moorland in County Durham, close to the wreckage of his taxi. He had been shot in the back of the head and his throat had been cut.

Back in Glasgow, Manuel's audacity was beyond belief. He willingly agreed to meet William Watt to discuss what had happened to his wife, daughter and sister-in-law. Watt was after justice. Manuel kept up his story of another man being responsible for the crimes. Watt and Manuel met on more than one occasion, Watt becoming increasingly convinced with each meeting that Manuel had killed his family.

In December the Platt family discovered some missing objects in the mattress that had been damaged in the robbery. They also discovered a bullet. It had come from the same gun as had been used in the Watt killings. Manuel's story about the same person committing the Platt robbery and the Watt killings was certainly true.

Later in the same month, Manuel robbed again. He broke into the home of the Houston family in Mount Vernon. Luckily, the Reverend Houston and his wife were out at the time.

Manuel's next murder was committed less than a week later. Isabelle Cooke, who lived very close to the Houston family, disappeared on her way to Uddingston to meet her boyfriend. Manuel had been careful to hide the body this time, and the police were unable to find out what had happened to her until much later.

Manuel's catalogue of violence was escalating. He killed again on 1 January 1958. The Smart family from Uddingston – Mr and Mrs Peter Smart and their eleven-year-old son, Michael – were found dead in their beds on 6 January. The last time Mr Smart had been seen alive was 31 December. Along with the macabre discovery of the bodies, police found evidence that the killer had spent time in the Smarts' house after he had murdered them. There were signs of him having eaten several meals on the premises. Not only that, but the family cat had been fed! Once again, it was as if Manuel was saying 'Come and find me'.

Public outrage and fear had reached a peak. Several people whose activities would normally make them want to steer well clear of the police came forward with information about Manuel. Manuel had been spending money freely in the early days of January. Some of this money was traced and the serial numbers on the notes coincided with the numbers of notes paid out to Mr Smart when he visited the bank on New Year's Eve. The police at once obtained a warrant to search the house where Manuel lived with his parents.

At last the net was closing in on Manuel. Vital evidence was found in the search that linked Manuel not only to the Smart killings but also to the robbery at the home of the Platt family in Bothwell Bridge and the robbery at the home of the Reverend

Houston and his family. Distinctive personal items that had been taken from the Platt and Houston homes were recovered at the Manuel house, along with some more of the banknotes that had been withdrawn from the bank by Mr Smart before he died. Both Peter Manuel and his father were arrested – Manuel's father was subsequently released.

Manuel went to some lengths to try to lie his way out of it, but the police had substantial evidence against him, and their persistent questioning finally wore him down. Perhaps, given his need for recognition, he wanted people to know what he had done. He confessed to the killings of the Smart family and to the break-ins at the Platt and Houston houses. In addition to this, he told the police that he was responsible for the Watt killings and the deaths of Anne Kneilands and Isabelle Cooke. He led the police to the spot where he had buried Isabelle Cooke, and they found her body, half-naked, buried beneath the soil. She had been strangled with her own bra.

There were two pieces of the jigsaw missing. In order to make the case against Manuel absolutely watertight, the police needed to find the two guns that he had used: the first to kill the Watt family and damage the mattress in the Platt's house; the second to kill the Smarts. Manuel told police officers that he had disposed of both guns in the River Clyde. A diver was sent down to search and, against all odds, eventually found first one weapon and then another on the river bed.

It seemed at this point as if Manuel had finally caved in. The investigating authorities had all the evidence that they needed to secure his conviction; they also had his confession. The trial was expected to proceed smoothly.

However, the showmanship of the killer had not been subdued. When the trial began in Glasgow on 12 May 1958, Manuel astounded the court by pleading not guilty to all the charges against him – eight counts of murder, three of housebreaking and one of theft. He accused William Watt of the killings of his family. For the other five murders, he claimed he had alibis. Manuel sat calmly in the dock as his bewildered lawyers proceeded with the case for his defence.

Four days later, Manuel stunned the court once again. He dismissed his counsel, claiming that he wanted to conduct his own defence.

It was not the first time that Manuel had done this. In 1955 he had appeared in court on a charge of rape and had insisted on defending himself. He had done this with remarkable success – the verdict of the jury had been not proven and Manuel had walked free.

Whether the decision to defend himself again was born of a hope that he could repeat his previous success in spite of the odds being heavily stacked against him, or whether he simply wished to revel in the attention that he would get from it all, Manuel caused a sensation.

The case went on for twelve more days, during which Manuel made every attempt to worm his way out of trouble. He persisted with his claim that William Watt was guilty of the Watt killings. He claimed he was a victim of a police conspiracy to frame him for the other crimes. He even tried to convince the court that Mr Smart had killed his own wife and son before committing suicide by shooting himself.

In spite of all his efforts – his skill in conducting his defence was reluctantly admitted by the judge in his summing up of the case – Manuel's claims lacked consistency and credibility. The jury did not take long to come to a decision, and in less than three hours, Manuel had been pronounced guilty of seven murders. The only charge upon which he was found not guilty was the murder of Anne Kneilands. There was not enough evidence to secure a conviction. The judge grimly sentenced Peter Thomas Anthony Manuel to death.

Manuel had not been made to answer for all of the atrocities for which he was responsible. He was not brought to trial for the murder of Sidney Dunn because this offence had not been committed in Scotland. Had Manuel's trial not turned out as expected and had he walked free, however, the Newcastle police were ready to arrest him. Now, of course, there was no need. Manuel was going to hang anyway.

While in prison awaiting execution, Manuel confessed to three more killings that had taken place, two in Glasgow, one in London, between 1954 and 1956. Many people believed that the tally did not stop there, but Manuel would say no more.

The date of execution had been set for 19 June, but after an unsuccessful appeal by Manuel, was finally set for Friday 11 July. Manuel became strangely silent in his final days. He tried to take his own life, by drinking disinfectant, but was unsuccessful. His fate was sealed.

Not long after eight o'clock in the morning on 11 July 1958, Peter Manuel was dead.

BIBLE JOHN

The stories of the killings in Glasgow that have been attributed to the man known as Bible John are well known. The killer has achieved notoriety similar to that of Jack the Ripper. To this day, in spite of all the efforts of the police, the identity of Bible John is unknown. He may be alive or dead. There are plenty of people who think they know who he was, or is. Somebody somewhere will probably harbour a suspicion too terrible to think about. But there is possibly no one, except the man himself, who knows for sure.

What is the picture that has been drawn up of this man?

In the course of their long and painstaking investigations, Glasgow police sought the assistance of a psychiatrist with many years of experience in studying the characteristics of serial killers. The profile with which the psychiatrist furnished the police suggested a number of possible traits that the killer might have.

He might be a woman-hater, finding it difficult to form proper relationships with members of the opposite sex. He might have limited sexual experience. He might have homosexual tendencies. The nature of his crimes suggested that he enjoyed the sense of power over the women whom he killed; perhaps the sexual component of the attacks was an assertion of his masculinity, which he felt to be somehow under threat.

The killer might well have been shy – a loner, or perhaps a bit of a mother's boy. Outwardly mild-mannered, he would also probably be very polite and quite prim and proper. All three of his victims were menstruating when they were killed. This fact seems to be too great a coincidence to be overlooked. Did the killer select them because they were menstruating (would they tell him before he raped them?) Or did he kill them because he discovered that they were menstruating when he raped them – did he believe that menstruating women were unclean? If this was the case, would the three girls have survived if they had not been menstruating?

Alone and in private, the killer would very possibly indulge his tastes for violence, particularly sexual violence, by reading violent and pornographic literature or watching erotic films at the cinema. It is unlikely that anyone else would be aware of these furtive habits.

The profile suggested some general tendencies that the killer might have but was by no means exact. What it did suggest, however, was that Bible John would be cunning enough to conceal carefully the perverted side of his nature from those who knew him. This is often the case with serial killers. The most striking characteristic about this man was likely to be his apparent ordinariness. This ordinariness, this ability to melt unnoticed into everyday society, is perhaps the reason why the man was never found.

It was 1968, the era of the dance halls in Glasgow. Saturday nights were the busiest, but the dance halls were able to make quite a decent profit during the week as well. If you wanted a good time, if you wanted to find a partner, the dance hall was the place to go. Dance halls were not only popular with single people. Married men and women would often go to these places for a good night out – many without the knowledge of their spouses. This was a factor that was thought to hamper police investigations into the three murders that took place between 1968 and 1969. Some people, who might have been in possession of information vital to the investigation, were in all probability prevented from coming forward because they risked being found out in adulterous activities by their husbands or wives.

The Barrowland Ballroom in Glasgow's east end was a popular venue. In February 1968, Bible John selected his first victim there. She was Patricia Docker, aged twenty-five. Her body was discovered, naked, on Friday 23 February, early in the morning. The body lay in a lane behind Carmichael Place, Langside. Patricia's home was very close by, in Langside Place. Patricia had been raped and strangled.

Patricia was a nursing auxiliary and worked in a hospital in Glasgow. She and her small son lived with her parents. She was estranged from her husband, who was serving in the army and stationed down south. She had gone out dancing with friends the night before but had never returned home. When she left home, she had been wearing an orange lacy dress and brown shoes. She had a grey coat and a brown handbag. She had told her parents that she was going to the Majestic Ballroom.

The Majestic Ballroom was in Hope Street. Over-twenty-fives' nights were held there, which were well attended by more mature revellers in Glasgow.

From the very beginning, the police found it hard to establish exactly what had happened to Patricia before she was killed. They questioned several people who had been at the Majestic on the night of 22 February, but they could not establish who had been the last to be in her company there or whom she had left with. Eventually they found out that she had moved on later in the evening from the Majestic to the Barrowland Ballroom.

Evidence was scant. It was thought that Pat had been killed somewhere else and her body moved to the lane where it was discovered. No trace of her clothes was ever found, in spite of meticulous searching in the surrounding area and in the waters of the River Cart. There had been a party in a flat overlooking the site where the body was found on the night of the 22nd, but although some of the people who had been at the party were nurses and knew Pat from work, Pat had not been there. Nor had anyone seen anything from the window of the flat or heard any suspicious noises outside.

The police continued their investigations for some months,

but in spite of their efforts, they got no further. The murder inquiry was eventually scaled down, but the case remained open.

The Barrowland Ballroom came to the attention of the Glasgow police once again, almost exactly eighteen months later. Mrs Margaret O'Brien had found the body of her sister hidden in a derelict tenement building in MacKeith Street. Her sister, Jemima MacDonald (Mima), had not returned after going out to the Barrowland Ballroom on the Saturday night. Mrs O'Brien had been searching for Mima when she had been alerted to the presence of something sinister in the empty building by some children who were playing nearby.

Mima O'Brien was thirty-two when she died. She had been severely beaten and strangled. She was fully clothed when she was found lying in the kitchen of one of the derelict flats. Her handbag, a black patent one, containing a brown purse, was nowhere to be seen. Her head scarf was also missing. The missing items were never found. The description that the police issued of Mima O'Brien in an attempt to trace her last movements contained the following details:

She was slim, about five foot seven inches tall.
Her hair was dyed brown, with fairer roots showing, and was shoulder length.
She was wearing a brown belted coat, over a black pinafore dress and white frilly blouse.
Her shoes were high-heeled slingbacks, off-white in colour.

Although Mima was not naked when she was found, her death had four things in common with that of Patricia Docker. Both women had been to the Barrowland Ballroom. Both women had been raped and strangled. Both women's bodies were found close to home. Finally, both women had been menstruating when they were killed.

The police got a little further with their investigations this time. They questioned people at the Barrowland Ballroom. They showed them photographs of Mima and asked whether her face was familiar. They needed to know who Mima had been dancing with and whether she had left the ballroom in the company of anyone. They were eventually able to gather quite a lot of information. Mima had been at the ballroom until around midnight, when she had left, accompanied by a tall man with reddish-fair hair. The couple had been seen turning into first Bain Street, then London Road, going towards Bridgeton Cross. Then they had gone on to MacKeith Street, via Landressy Street and James Street.

The man seen with Mima was about six foot two inches tall, in his late twenties to early thirties, and was well dressed, wearing a blue suit and a white shirt.

The police mounted a reconstruction of events leading up to Mima's death. They hoped that someone might see it and remember something else that might help them with the investigation. Unfortunately, it did not get them much further forward. In spite of taking the unprecedented step of having an Identikit picture of the suspected killer published in the press, the police got no further in their search.

The killer struck again, on Thursday 31 October. It was after this third killing that the murderer became known as Bible John. The body of Helen Puttock was found in the early hours of the following day. She was lying, face down, in a back court in Earl Street in Scotstoun. A man came upon the body when his dog started sniffing around the gruesome heap.

Like Mima, Helen was still wearing the clothes she had left to go dancing in – a black dress and a fur coat. Her handbag had gone and was never found. Like both Mima and Pat, she was found close to home. Once again, the killer had found a woman who was menstruating. Helen's sanitary towel was found tucked under her arm. Was the killer trying to make a point? The killing had followed a similar course to the previous two; Helen Puttock had been raped and strangled.

Helen had gone to the Barrowland Ballroom on the Thursday night with her sister, Mrs Jean Langford. The two women had been together until shortly before Helen had been killed, and Jean Langford was able to supply the police with vital evidence. She had seen her sister's suspected killer. She had talked to him and shared a taxi home.

Helen had started talking to the man when he had helped her at the dance hall with a cigarette machine that had refused to work. The two had got along famously. Helen had accepted a drink from the stranger, who told her his name was John, and they had danced together.

At the end of the evening, John and another man, also called John, had left with Helen and Jean. Helen's John had been quite insistent that the two women should not travel home unaccompanied and suggested that they share a taxi. The other John had departed, and Helen, her new-found friend and her sister had hailed a taxi together at Glasgow Cross.

Both women had been very impressed by John's solicitous manner and his obvious charm. He was smartly dressed and quite handsome. He seemed to talk quite freely about himself but managed to avoid going into any detail. He told the girls that he came from a strictly religious background. He himself was teetotal, but he did not share his parents' religious beliefs. As a consequence of his religious upbringing, he was able to recite passages from the Bible by heart. In the course of his conversation with the two sisters, he made references to the Bible. John did not say what he did for a living, saying only that he worked in a laboratory. Certainly, in dress, demeanour and conversation, he did not give the impression that he was a labourer or manual worker.

How much of the information that the killer gave away about himself that night was true? It could all have been an elaborate facade, after all, to send investigating officers off on a trail to nowhere, leaving him free to do as he wished. Bible John almost certainly intended to have sexual relations with Helen Puttock that night. He probably knew the encounter was going to end in death. The presence of her sister presented him with a problem; it meant that he risked detection. But what if he took that risk specifically to direct the investigations of the police into this and his previous two killings to send them off at a tangent? Was he as clever as this?

Jean Langford had been every bit as charmed by their new acquaintance as her sister, and she felt no qualms about leaving Helen alone in the taxi with John when she got out at her own home, which was in Knightswood. The last sighting of Helen and Bible John was in Scotstoun, at around 12.30 a.m. on Friday 31 October.

The details that Jean Langford gave to the police were gathered together and used to issue the following statement to the press, describing the man that the police were looking for.

He is about twenty-five to twenty-nine years of age, five foot ten inches to six feet in height, and is of medium build. He has light auburn, reddish hair, brushed to the right. He has blue-grey eyes and nice straight teeth, but one tooth on the upper right overlaps the next.

He has fine features and is generally of a smart, modern appearance. This man was known to be dressed in a brownish, flecked, single-breasted suit with high lapels. His brownish coat – tweed or gabardine – was worn knee-length.

His wristwatch has a military style strap – a thick strap with a thinner strap linked through it.

He may smoke Embassy tipped cigarettes and goes to the Barrowland Ballroom. He is thought to be called by the Christian name John. He may speak of having a strict upbringing and make references to the Bible.

This man is quite well spoken, probably with a Glasgow accent, and there may be marks on his face and hands.

The description got a good response from the public and gave the police information on one more probable sighting of Bible John, on a bus in the early hours of the morning. As had been suspected might be the case – there was evidence to suggest that Helen Puttock had put up a struggle and might have scratched her killer – the man on the bus had a bright red mark on his face and his clothes were dirty and dishevelled.

The police stepped up the pace of their inquiries now. Fear was mounting in the community; there could be no doubt that the three women who had been killed in the past twenty-two months had been victims of the same man. This man was a clever and cold-hearted killer. There was every likelihood that he would strike again. Pressure increased to find the murderer.

Policemen visited dance halls all over Glasgow and some went undercover in the Barrowland Ballroom, dancing with the regular attenders, all the time keeping their eyes on the clientele, hoping to catch a glimpse of Bible John. People from all walks of life were questioned and extensive door-to-door inquiries were carried out. Suspects were brought in for questioning and then released. Some of them were brought in again – and again. Suspicions fell on men from all walks of life, including members of the police and the army. Countless people were interviewed, either as suspects or as potential witnesses. In desperation, the police called on the services of a psychic, a Dutchman called Gerard Croiset. Croiset furnished the police with some leads as to where he believed the killer might be found – he was convinced that Bible John was still in Glasgow – but in the end, the trail went cold.

Nearly forty years later the mystery of Bible John continues to haunt the Glasgow constabulary.

Why were there no more killings? Did the killer leave the country? Did he die? Did he decide for some reason known only to himself that he could, or must now, stop? Or had Bible John been incarcerated for some other crime? Any of the above was possible.

The case still rankles, and as recently as 1996, steps were taken to disinter the body of one man who had once been a suspect in the hope that DNA testing might identify him as having been the killer. The man had committed suicide in 1980. He had had red hair, like the killer. He had been at the Barrowland Ballroom. He came from a strictly religious background. Could he have been Bible John? The investigations must have caused a great deal of pain for the family of the dead man and, in the end, it was all for nothing. Once again, the police drew a blank.

Everybody who had any involvement in the case of Bible John has a theory. Some believe that Bible John is still alive somewhere, a man of about sixty now, with a dark secret. Others believe that he must be dead. The one thing that everybody finds hardest to believe is that there is not someone, somewhere, who knows the truth.

THOMAS ROSS YOUNG

In October 1977, Thomas Ross Young, a lorry driver from Glasgow, was sentenced to two life terms for a horrific catalogue of violence, including a murder, which he had carried out over a period of approximately two years. Young had been imprisoned for acts of violence in the past: in 1967 he had been sentenced to eighteen months in prison for rape and in 1969 he was sentenced to eight years, again for rape. His criminal history stretched back to childhood, and his first conviction for a sexual offence was when he was thirteen, when he was found guilty of indecent assault and theft.

Young had had a disturbed childhood. He was illegitimate, and his mother, unwilling to shoulder the responsibility of bringing up a child, left him in the care of his grandparents, who eventually adopted him when he was eleven. He was only nine years old when he first got into trouble with the police, the first of several encounters with the law over the following years.

He married in 1956, and his wife, Alice, suffered repeated acts of severe violence at his hands throughout their time together until she finally divorced him in 1973. The couple had three sons and one daughter. Young was as vicious in his treatment of his sons as he was with his wife. The only member of the family who was not subjected to physical assault was his daughter, upon whom he doted.

Thomas Young's sexual appetite was voracious and he was repeatedly unfaithful to his wife during the seventeen years that they were married. She was painfully aware that he was having relations with other women; he might have concealed the fact that he was married from the women he met, but he was less careful when it came to hiding his extramarital affairs from Alice. She was powerless to object.

In 1967, when Young was working as a lorry driver, he came under suspicion when a girl called Pat McAdam from Dumfries disappeared. She had been hitching home after a trip to Glasgow with a friend, and they had been picked up by a lorry driver. Pat's friend had been dropped off in Annan, where she lived. Pat was never seen again.

Police investigations revealed that Thomas Ross Young was the lorry driver who had picked Pat and her friend up but could take the matter no further as they had no evidence to link Young with Pat's disappearance. Young admitted to having given the girls a lift but maintained that he had dropped Pat off when they reached Dumfries. Pat's body was never found, and the investigation was eventually wound down.

In the same year Young found himself in court in England, accused of rape. His victim was nineteen years old. He was sentenced to eighteen months in prison for the offence.

In 1970 Young was in trouble again. He received an eight-year sentence, this time, for the rape of a fifteen-year-old girl. The offence had taken place in his lorry, somewhere in Lanarkshire. This was the point at which his wife, who had suffered so much for so long, initiated proceedings for divorce.

In 1975 Young was released from prison again. He found himself a flat in Glasgow and returned to long-distance lorry driving. He returned to his violent ways as well, with renewed ferocity. Lorry driving was the perfect job for a man like Young. He could pick up girls all over the country and use them to satisfy his sexual appetite. The exact number of girls with whom Young had intercourse in the cab of his lorry can only be guessed at, but, inevitably, not all of them were willing partners. Thomas Young had used violence so many times before that he did not hesitate to use it again. For two years Young remained free to do as he pleased. He found women wherever he was, whether he was working in his lorry or at home, with his car for transport on days off. After his arrest he told the police how easy it all was. His record with the company for whom he worked was faultless. He was neat, clean, punctual and reliable. What Young did in his spare time was of no interest to his employers and whatever he got up to in the cab of his lorry remained a secret.

It was 1977 before the police finally found themselves on his trail. In April a prostitute reported to police that she had been attacked by a lorry driver. She had taken the man as a client, but he had refused to pay and had raped her and beaten her with a metal bar to her severe injury. Luckily, she had escaped and been given assistance by the driver of a passing car.

Then in June the body of a thirty-seven-year-old woman was found on a small country road in Glenboig. The body was in a state of decomposition. It was lying face down, hidden in some shrubbery at the side of the road. The woman had been bound with her hands behind her back. Her pants had been stuffed into her mouth. She had died from strangulation. Her name was Frances Barker and she had been missing from her home in Glasgow for over two weeks. She was thought to have accepted a lift from a stranger on the day she went missing.

The body of Frances Barker had been found on the same road as the one where the prostitute had been attacked. The police suspected that they were looking for the same man for both crimes. The investigation rapidly gained momentum. Dates and times and places were checked and double-checked. Haulage companies were investigated. The routes of the drivers were checked and double-checked. Descriptions were cross-checked and a catalogue of brutal sexual assaults were soon linked together. The link was Thomas Young.

Young knew that he was being pursued by the police. He was desperate. He had never lost contact with his former wife. Now he returned to her house to torment her one last time. He punched her and threatened to kill her unless she hid him. In real fear for her life, she had no choice.

The police suspected that Young might be hiding out at his former wife's home. Day and night they kept watch on it. Finally their patience was rewarded when they caught sight of Young at a window. They moved swiftly in on their prey and soon Young was locked up.

The evidence that the police had so far was not enough to convict Thomas Young of all the crimes of which they suspected him. The forensic team set to work at once, combing Young's lorry, his car, his flat and his former wife's flat for vital evidence. One of the most telling pieces of evidence that was found was a bracelet that Young had given his daughter. It had belonged to Frances Barker.

After his arrest, Young confessed to the police but denied having made the confession when his case was tried. His behaviour was bizarre. He raged at police officers, demanding help, denying responsibility for his actions. Shortly afterwards, he adopted an attitude of cold silence, which he was to maintain throughout his subsequent trial. He was a frightening figure.

Feeling sure that this man had committed more offences than the ones with which they had charged him, the police investigated other unsolved crimes that might be linked with Young and questioned him once more about the disappearance of Pat McAdam in 1967. They got no further in spite of their efforts, but by now they were confident that they had sufficient evidence linking Young to a horrifying catalogue of violence to ensure that he was put away for a very long time.

The trial took place in October, barely four months after Frances Barker was killed.

Thomas Young was charged with the following crimes:

The murder of Frances Barker

The rape and attempted murder of the prostitute in Glenboig

The rape and assault of a sixteen-year-old girl in his own home

The rape at knife point of a prostitute in Waterloo Street car park in Glasgow

The rape, assault and robbery of a sixty-five-year-old woman

Assault on a twenty-year-old woman in Carntyne

Assault on a prostitute with a lighted cigarette

Assault on a prostitute at Charing Cross

The rape of a woman in Paisley

Assault on his wife

He was found not guilty on three charges: the rape of the pensioner, the assault at Charing Cross and the Paisley rape. On one charge – assaulting a prostitute with a cigarette – the case against him was not proven. On all other counts he was found guilty as charged. He was sentenced to two terms of life imprisonment.

THE CASE OF SHEILA GARVIE

Sheila Garvie, born Sheila Watson, had a window onto the lives of the privileged. Her father worked on the royal estate at Balmoral for some years and Sheila spent her adolescence there. She worked in the castle itself for a while, as a maid, not long after she left school. Then the family moved to Stonehaven and Sheila found work in Aberdeen. In 1954 she met the man who was to become her husband – Max Garvie – at a local dance. The couple married less than a year later, in June 1955. Sheila was only eighteen, but the marriage earned her parents' approval. Max Garvie was a farmer, quite a catch for a lass like Sheila. He was prosperous and good-looking, and the two seemed set for a contented life together in the farmhouse in Kincardineshire.

All was not quite as rosy for the young bride as might have appeared to outsiders, however. What had started off as a match that seemed to be made in heaven gradually turned, over a period of years, into the marriage from hell for Sheila Garvie.

Max Garvie was very much a man of the swinging sixties. His appetite for sex was considerable and his activities in that sphere were not always of a nature that Sheila found tasteful. In private, his demands on Sheila in the bedroom were becoming increasingly out of the ordinary. He started a collection of pornographic literature and took great pleasure in poring over every detail. Fuelled by what he read, he was constantly looking for new ways to find a sexual thrill.

His eagerness to experiment with his wife was not reciprocated, especially as his tastes veered from the daring to the deviant.

Publicly, Max became very enthusiastic about nudism, but less in the naturist than in the voyeuristic sense. He even set up facilities for nudists on his own property. The couple had three children, two of whom were girls, and Max was disturbingly persistent in his attempts to persuade Sheila that the girls should also take part in visits to nudist camps that he coerced her into.

As his desire to spice up his sex life moved up a gear, Max introduced Sheila to Brian Tevendale. In order to satisfy his own voyeuristic desires, Max wanted his wife to take up a sexual relationship with Brian, but Brian, a long-standing acquaintance of Max's, was not aware of this. Max would invite Brian to his home and engineer opportunities for him and Sheila to be alone together. Over a period of time, Sheila was given every opportunity and encouragement to have sex with Tevendale. Eventually she relented. Unknown to Max, Sheila gave in not because of Max's wishes, but because, over time, she and Tevendale had found themselves genuinely attracted to one another. To have a relationship with Brian suited Sheila as much as it suited Max.

It was autumn 1967. Max was quite thrilled; he enjoyed the presence of a third party in his relationship with Sheila. It excited him. Moreover, his interest in Tevendale did not stop with the young man's liaison with his wife. Max wanted a physical relationship with Tevendale himself. In this, he was disappointed. Tevendale was not interested at all. He did, however, introduce Max to a fourth party – Trudy Birse, his sister. This certainly added spice to Garvie's life. He was immediately attracted to her and embarked upon a sexual relationship with her with considerable enthusiasm. Tevendale, Birse and the Garvies became a foursome, with Max Garvie getting his thrills from having sex with both Sheila and Trudy and also vicariously from hearing every intimate detail of Sheila's relationship with Tevendale. Sheila did not like the arrangement particularly, but she tolerated it as long as she got a chance to be together with Brian Tevendale.

These arrangements were all very well for Max Garvie as long as he was in control, manipulating the other three towards his own ends. After a while, however, it became clear that Sheila and Brian had more than a sexual relationship going on. This made him extremely angry and jealous. He became violent towards Sheila and demanded that she finish with Tevendale. She refused. Max retaliated with threats and violence, both towards Tevendale and Sheila. It was a turbulent time. Sheila was desperately unhappy and told her mother and some others about her plight. Sad to say, she did not get the support that she needed to escape her marriage.

Then in May 1968 Max Garvie disappeared. He was last seen alive in the middle of May. Max's wild living, his liking for alcohol and drugs and his taste for pornography were quite common knowledge. Nobody suspected that he might have been killed. Most people who knew him thought that he had simply run off – most likely with a woman. Not long after Max had been reported missing, Sheila and Brian Tevendale began to be seen together frequently, obviously enjoying each other's company, quite open in their affection for one another.

There were no real whispers of suspected foul play on Sheila's part, however, until August. This was when Sheila Garvie's mother took herself to the police to voice some suspicions that she had about her daughter. Sheila had told her mother that Max Garvie would not be back. She said that he was dead and gave a clear impression that Brian Tevendale knew something about what had happened. She asked her mother about tidal currents, giving her mother the feeling that Max's body had probably been disposed of at sea. Sheila also told her mother that she intended to start a new life with Tevendale. Sheila Garvie's mother, who had known for some time of her daughter's terrible unhappiness in her marriage to Max, feared the worst. Sheila had not told her in so many words

173

that Max had been murdered, but it was the obvious conclusion to come to.

On 16 August Sheila Garvie and Brian Tevendale were arrested in connection with the disappearance of Max Garvie. Another man, Alan Peters, was arrested along with them, believed to be an accomplice of Tevendale's.

Tevendale quickly admitted that Max Garvie was dead and agreed to take the police to where the body had been left. His version of the story was that he was innocent of the murder. Sheila had killed Max Garvie. Garvie had been trying to coerce her into having anal intercourse and had threatened her with a rifle. She had refused to comply with Garvie's wishes and in the ensuing struggle, the rifle had gone off and Garvie had been killed. Sheila had then phoned Tevendale in a state of panic and he had helped her to conceal the body.

This story was supposed to get Tevendale off the murder charge he was facing. As long as Sheila related the same version of events he was in the clear. He led the investigating team of policemen to a tunnel leading from Lauriston Castle where they found the body of Max Garvie. He had been shot in the neck. He also had a fractured skull.

Tevendale's story began to lack credibility almost immediately. His sister, Trudy, when she was interviewed by the police, told them that Tevendale had given her another version of events. Tevendale had told his sister that he had gone to the Garvie farmhouse with Alan Peters, and it was Alan Peters who had struck Garvie on the head with an iron bar. Tevendale had then shot him. The two men had hidden the body together.

Then there was the statement that Alan Peters gave to the police. It was different again. Alan Peters said that he and Tevendale had gone to the Garvie house together. Tevendale had picked up the gun after entering the house. Sheila Garvie had given Tevendale and himself a drink while they waited for Max Garvie to go to bed.

After some time Sheila had reported that her husband was asleep, and then she had shown the two men up to the bedroom where Max Garvie was sleeping. Tevendale had gone up to the sleeping man, struck him on the head with the butt of the rifle and then shot him. Peters admitted to having assisted in the disposal of the body but not to having taken any active part in the killing. Tevendale had done the killing with Sheila as his accomplice.

Sheila Garvie told yet another story. According to her statement, she had been in bed with her husband when she had been woken by Tevendale, accompanied by another man, pulling her out of bed by the arm. Tevendale had steered her into the bathroom and told her to stay put. He had been carrying a gun. As she waited in the bathroom, Sheila claimed to have heard thumping noises coming from the bedroom. After a few minutes, Tevendale had come back and told her to keep watch outside the children's bedroom door in case they woke up. Tevendale turned back to Max Garvie's bedroom and shortly emerged with his companion, dragging the body of her husband, wrapped in some bedclothes, behind them.

Four different stories in total, implicating three people in different ways. Which one of them had carried out the killing – Sheila Garvie, Brian Tevendale or Alan Peters?

The trial took place at the High Court in Aberdeen, starting on 19 November 1968 and attracting nationwide media coverage. The public were intrigued by the story of Max Garvie and his sexual appetites. It was quite a sensation. Those closer to the case, however, found the process a very painful one. Sheila Garvie's mother, a principal witness for the prosecution, was seen to be in considerable distress. Sheila herself seemed tired, very weak and extremely depressed. As details of the miserable marriage to Max that Sheila felt forced to endure emerged, there was more than a little sympathy for her amongst those who filled the courtroom. Her mother told how she knew that Max treated her daughter badly, coercing her into indulging his distasteful sexual whims with bullying and, at times,

175

violence. A minister whom Sheila had approached for help and advice related how she had told him much the same sort of thing as she had told her mother. He had urged her to stick to her marriage vows. Nowadays, nearly forty years on, we can freely condemn both Sheila's mother and the minister for acting as they did in response to her pleas for help. They told her, more or less, to go back to Garvie, to stay with him, to make the best of a bad job. Sheila was made to feel that there was no way out for her. But forty years ago, things were different. It may have been the swinging sixties and the age of sexual permissiveness, but there was still a great stigma attached to divorce. Sheila's mother probably thought that she was acting in the best interests of her daughter in the long run. Sheila had made her bed and now must lie on it, however painful it might be. Had it all taken place forty years on, it might all have turned out another way. Sheila might have been strong enough and might have had the support she needed to leave Max. He might have lived.

All three defendants pleaded not guilty to murder. The defence teams did their best. Sheila Garvie's defence in particular, Lionel Daiches QC, made a powerful plea on her behalf.

Alan Peters' defence maintained that he had helped to conceal the body of Max Garvie because he was afraid of Brian Tevendale. Peters himself took the witness stand and told the jury how he feared for his own life at Tevendale's hands if he refused to help him. He stuck to his denial of having played any active part in the killing itself.

Tevendale opted not to give evidence on his own behalf. The case for his defence was already much weaker than those of Sheila Garvie or Alan Peters, for he had already been found to have lied at least once about what happened on the night of the killing.

Sheila's defence made much of the fact that Max Garvie had been a manipulative, bullying man with unnatural sexual appetites and that Sheila had been trapped in a loveless marriage.

Her relationship with Tevendale had brought her closer to happiness, and it was understandable, if not justifiable, that she should feel compelled to help Tevendale in any way she could by keeping quiet about his killing of Garvie.

Whilst there was genuine sympathy for Sheila's predicament in her marriage to Max, the jury was still faced with the decision as to whether or not she had assisted in any way with the murder. The decision was really based on the answer to one question. Had Sheila Garvie let Tevendale and Peters into the farmhouse, waited until Max was asleep and then shown them upstairs, as Peters' version of events told? Or had Tevendale taken the decision to kill Garvie upon himself without her prior knowledge, as Sheila claimed?

The case against Brian Tevendale was carried. He was found guilty of murder by a unanimous verdict.

Alan Peters fared better. The case against him was found not proven.

Sheila Garvie was found guilty, along with Brian Tevendale, of the murder of her husband. The verdict of the jury in her case was not unanimous.

Some ten years later, both Sheila Garvie and Brian Tevendale were released from prison, within months of each other. Their passion for each other, ignited and fuelled by the difficult circumstances under which they met, had long since died out. They had corresponded for a while from their prison cells, but their relationship ground to a halt. Upon their release from prison, they each got on with their own, very separate lives.

THE WORLD'S END MURDERS: CHRISTINE EADIE AND HELEN SCOTT

It was 15 October 1977. The long days of summer were at an end and autumn had come to Scotland's capital city. The nights were closing in and in a few days' time, the clocks would change: the official recognition of the approach of winter. But if there was an ominous chill in the air that evening, Christine Eadie and Helen Scott were not caring. It was Saturday night. They were both seventeen. They had both left school and were working now, and they were enjoying the sense of freedom that the prospect of a weekend off with money in their purses gave them. It was time to have fun.

The two teenagers had been close friends since childhood and their friendship had continued uninterrupted after they had left school. Tragically, their outing on 15 October was to be the last of their joint exploits.

The World's End, a pub on the corner of St Mary's Street and the Royal Mile in the centre of the city, was busy that night. Christine and Helen settled down with their friends and ordered their first round of drinks. Before long, all the girls were getting into the swing of the evening, drinking, laughing, joking and having a good time.

During the course of the evening, two men approached Christine and Helen and engaged them in conversation. The men seemed to be a few years older than the girls – in their twenties at least, perhaps as old as thirty. The girls seemed to be flattered by the attentions of the two men – where is the harm in being chatted up on a night out when you have your friends there for moral support? Emboldened by drink and high spirits, Christine and Helen willingly joined in the banter. The men bought the girls drinks and joined them at their table.

After a while, the girls who had been with Christine and Helen left the pub. When they left, their two friends were still talking to their new acquaintances. At around 11.15 p.m., Christine and Helen finally left the pub. It was the last time the two girls were seen alive.

The next day, two grim discoveries were made in East Lothian, about fifteen miles from Edinburgh. On the stretch of coastline between Longniddry and Aberlady, at a place called Gosford Bay, the body of Christine was the first to be found. Two Sunday walkers came across the dead girl early in the afternoon. She was lying in the open, scarcely concealed by the sand dunes, her hands tied behind her back. She had been stripped of all her clothes, brutally beaten, sexually assaulted and strangled. Her best friend's body was found a few hours later, some five or six miles away, in a field near Haddington. She had been treated in the same callous way as Christine – stripped, beaten, sexually assaulted and strangled.

The murders sparked off a massive hunt for the killers, with the two men who had left the World's End pub with Christine and Helen as the prime suspects. There had been plenty of people in the pub that night. The girls' friends had been able to provide descriptions of the two men to the police to help them to make up Photofit pictures. Surely someone would be able to come forward with a name or two, or a clue as to the identities of the suspects. As teams of men and tracker dogs scoured East Lothian for forensic evidence, an appeal went out to all those who had been in the World's End on the night of Saturday 15 October.

It is surprising to realise that while alcohol can turn strangers into warm acquaintances who will happily keep company in the warm, friendly atmosphere of the pub on a Saturday night, buying each other drinks, swapping stories and sharing jokes as if they had known each other all their lives, the cold air of sobriety on the morning after brings with it estrangement and silence.

Comparatively few people were willing to come forward to help the police with their inquiries. Certainly, fewer people came forward than the many who must have seen both the two men and the girls. Painstakingly, the police followed every possible lead, taking detailed statements from witnesses, trawling through the pubs of Edinburgh searching for someone who might recognise either or both of the men, even if from another pub on another night. Investigations in the area where the girls' bodies were found came up with a possible sighting of Helen in a car in the early hours of Sunday morning, but it was no more than that – a possible sighting. It took detectives no further forward. Items of clothing were found by the teams of searchers, but they yielded no evidence that would help the police until they had at least one suspect in custody.

The girls had not been killed where their bodies were found. They had been killed elsewhere and then dumped – quite carelessly. Where had the killings taken place? Again, the police were unable to discover anything. And what had been the primary motive for the killings? Had it been the desire to silence the girls after they had been raped or did the killer, or killers, seek the thrill of the violence and death as much as the sexual acts? The girls' handbags had gone and were never found, but robbery could never have been the motive. The degree of violence that had been inflicted and the sexual element of the attacks left this in no doubt.

It was a crime that the police believed they ought to be able to solve. They had two suspects to look for after all – this meant two opportunities for positive identification by witnesses. If one suspect could be identified, the other could certainly be found.

Investigating officers had what they thought were good descriptions of the suspects. The Photofit ought to have jogged someone's memory. With the possibility that both men had been involved, there was a chance that one of them might give himself away somehow, either through carelessness or after giving way under the pressure of guilt. From the forensic evidence available at the time, it was thought that possibly only one of the pair had been responsible for all, or most, of the violence. If this was the case, then perhaps the other had been coerced into playing his part in the abductions and killings rather than being a willing accomplice. Might he find the courage to come forward? Or perhaps after all there was only one killer and the two suspects in the pub were simply what they had seemed, two men having a good night out?

The months passed and the police got nowhere. Gradually the intensity of the murder investigation diminished. Occasionally there was a spark of hope as some small clue emerged. A couple of anonymous letters claiming knowledge of the identity of the culprits were followed up, but both led to dead ends.

There are always other crimes to deal with, and after several months of intense and highly pressured work, the police found themselves in a position where there was no longer enough new evidence to justify maintaining the murder inquiry at more than a minimum level.

However, the case was not forgotten – no unsolved murder is – and the file on the World's End killings had remained open for almost thirty years when in 2004 senior detectives from Lothian and Borders police, Strathclyde police and Tayside police launched Operation Trinity to re-examine the World's End murders along with some other unsolved murders that occurred during the period 1977 to 1980.

New DNA evidence provided the breakthrough that was needed to solve Scotland's longest murder investigation and finally, in 2005, it emerged that a man had appeared in court in connection with the murder of the two girls, which it was hoped might bring closure to the twenty-nine-year-old investigation. However, his trial collapsed in 2007 when the judge ruled that there was not enough evidence to convict him.

THE ULTIMATE PENALTY

Capital punishment was finally abolished in Great Britain in 1969. The sentence for murder is now life imprisonment. 'Life' does not generally mean a life spent behind bars, for a 'lifer' can expect, with good behaviour, to be released from prison after as little as ten years. A lifer can never be free, however, for he or she is only released on licence. The slightest transgression can mean a return to confinement.

The debate as to whether capital punishment should be restored continues, and the question is raised in parliament from time to time. There is also a strong body of opinion in favour of keeping most, if not all, convicted murderers locked up for the rest of their natural lives.

Apart from the argument that it is wrong in any circumstances to take a life, those who argue that the death penalty should not be restored maintain that the possibility that someone might be convicted and hanged in error is too real to be ignored. Whilst across the Atlantic, in the United States of America, opinion is moving in the opposite direction and recent years have seen an increase in the numbers of those held on death row and of those who have been executed, the British government still stands firm.

Executions were, in times gone by, relatively commonplace. They were not always carried out humanely, and in the days when they were public they made a horrifying and brutal spectacle. You did not have to be a murderer to suffer the death penalty. In the early part of the nineteenth century several people were hanged for robbery in Scotland – seven between 1830 and 1831 alone.

Gradually the brutality of the system was ameliorated. Murder became the only crime for which a person could be hanged. Public executions were abolished. Fewer and fewer people suffered the death penalty for murder until, finally, capital punishment was abolished altogether.

A brief look at the facts about executions in Scotland for murder can be very thought-provoking.

Between 1750 and 1800, seventeen women were executed for murder. Of these seventeen women, twelve had killed their own children, most of whom had been illegitimate babies. In the same period of time, thirty-six men were executed for murder.

The last execution in Scotland for murder was carried out in Aberdeen on 15 August 1963. It was the first execution in the granite city for over one hundred years. Henry John Burnett, aged twenty-one, was hanged for shooting Thomas Geujan, twenty-seven, to death. Burnett had been having an affair with Geujan's wife, Margaret.

The last public execution in Scotland was that of nineteen-year-old Robert Smith in Dumfries on 12 May 1868. Robert Smith had been tried and convicted of the rape, robbery and murder of a nine-year-old girl and an assault on another woman.

The first private execution for murder took place in Perth. A forty-five-year-old man, George Chalmers, was found guilty of robbing and murdering John Miller of the Blackhill Toll Bar, Braco, in 1869. Sentence was carried out on 4 October 1870.

Until the early 1830s it was quite commonplace for the bodies of executed murderers to be given up for dissection. Such was the fate that befell the corpse of William Burke. The last body that he provided for the surgeons of Edinburgh was his own.

The last woman to be executed for murder in Scotland was Susan Newell. Newell had killed a thirteen-year-old boy, Johnnie Johnstone, and the crime was discovered as Newell tried to move the child's body from Coatbridge to Glasgow to dispose of it.

Pleas of insanity by her defence team were dismissed and Newell was condemned to death. She was hanged in Glasgow on 10 October 1923. She was the first woman to be executed in Scotland in over thirty years. The woman who was executed before her was Jessie King, hanged in Edinburgh in 1889 for the murder of two small children in her care. Newell was the only woman to be hanged in Scotland in the twentieth century.

The last hanging in Edinburgh was that of George Robertson, who was executed in June 1954 for the murder of his ex-wife, Elizabeth.

Anthony Joseph Miller's was the last execution that Glasgow saw. He was hanged in 1960 for the murder and robbery of a man called John Cremin.

In the second half of the eighteenth century, a total of eighty-six people were executed for murder in Scotland. The first half of the nineteenth century saw ninety go to the scaffold for murder. The twentieth century compares with only twenty-three people being executed between 1900 and 1950.

Of the ninety people who were hanged in the first half of the nineteenth century, seventy-nine were men and eleven were women. Out of the seventy-nine men, twenty-four had killed their own wives or lovers. Four of the eleven women had killed their husbands.

INDEX

A. B. 113, 114
Aberdeen 89, 147, 171, 175
Aberfeldy 145, 146
Aberlady 179
Adams, Arthur 98–101, 102, 103, 105, 113
Adams, Dr 101, 109
Aitchison KC, Craigie 116, 140
Aitken, James 87, 88
Anderson, Adolf 98, 103
Annan 167
Annandale, John see Laurie, John Watson
Antoine, Madame Andrée Junio 98, 103, 104, 107, 110
Antwerp 130
Ardlamont 6, 90–96
Argyll 151
Arran 83–89
Assynt 24
Bain Street, Glasgow 161
Baird, Robert 30
Balmoral 171
Banks family 80
Barker, Frances 168, 169, 170
Barlinnie Prison 149
Barrowland Ballroom 158, 159, 160, 161, 162, 163, 164, 165
Barrowman, Mary 102, 103, 105, 112, 116
Battley's Sedative Solution 68, 71
Bean Family 8–11

Berkeley Street, Glasgow 64, 65, 66
Bible John 157–165
Birrel, Miss 113, 114
Birse, Trudy 172, 174
Blackhill Toll Bar, Braco 184
Blackstock, Dr 119
Blythswood Drive, Glasgow 113
Blythswood Square, Glasgow 35, 36
body-snatching 17–23
Bonnar, Isobel Veronica see Merret, Vera
Bonnar, Mrs 140, 141, 143
Bothwell, Earl of 15, 16
Bothwell Bridge 152, 153
Braco 184
Bridge of Allan 40, 41, 42, 43, 45, 50, 51
Bridge Street Station, Glasgow 57
Bridgend 118
Bridgeton Cross, Glasgow 161
Brodick 86
Broom, Loch 24
Broomielaw, Glasgow 56, 58
Broughty Ferry 111, 112, 124–131
Brown, Janet 20
Brown, Margaret 151
Buccleuch, Duke of 118
Buchan 147
Buchanan, Mary Jane 41
Buckingham Terrace, Edinburgh 135, 139
Burke, William 17–23, 184
Burley, Sergeant 121

Burnett, Henry John 184

Bute, Isle of 83, 84, 85, 86, 87

Calton Hill, Edinburgh 134

Calton Prison 77, 82, 133

Campbell, Elizabeth 79, 81

Campbell, Mrs 56, 57

Canonmills, Edinburgh 79

capital punishment 183–185 *see also* hangings

Carmichael Place, Glasgow 159

Carntyne, Glasgow 170

Cart, River 159

Chalmers, George 184

Chantrelle, Elizabeth (née Cullen Dyer) 74–77

Chantrelle, Eugene Marie 73–77, 134

Charing Cross, Glasgow 41, 170

Charlotte Square, Edinburgh 96

Chesney, Ronald *see* Merret, John Donald

Cheyne Street, Edinburgh 80

Christie, Betty 136, 137, 138

Clapperton, Alec 119, 120, 121

Clapperton, Mary 119

Clyde, River 154

Coatbridge 84

College of Surgeons 63

Cook, David 112, 115

Cooke, Isabelle 153, 154

Corrie, Alfred 118, 122–123

Corrie Hotel, Arran 86

Covenanters 5

Cowan, Dr James 67

Cremin, John 185

Croiset, Gerard 164

Currie's (chemist's) 41, 42

'Daft Jamie' 21

Daiches QC, Lionel 176

Dalkeith 118–123

Dalkeith Road, Edinburgh 79

Dallas, John 23

dance halls 158, 164

Darnley, Lord 12–16

Davidson and Syme 96

de Mean, Auguste 44

Deas, Lord 59

Docherty, Mrs 21, 22

Docker, Patricia 158, 159, 160, 161

Dornoch Jail 27, 28

Douglas, Earl of 14

Douglas, Superintendent 113, 114

Doyle, Sir Arthur Conan 111, 115, 116

Drumbeg 25

Dumfries 167, 184

Dunbar 15

Dundee 49, 125

Dunedin Palais de Danse, Edinburgh 136

Dunn, Sidney 149, 152, 155

Dunoon 54

Dyer, Elizabeth Cullen *see* Chantrelle, Elizabeth

Eadie, Christine 178–182

Earl Street, Glasgow 161

East Kilbride 150

East Lothian 179

Edinburgh 10, 15, 16, 17, 19, 20, 21, 22, 32, 42, 46, 49, 64, 66, 70, 73, 77, 79, 89, 96, 106, 119, 134, 135, 138, 139, 184, 185

Elizabeth I, Queen 12, 15

Elmgrove House 124–131

Falkirk 21

Fennsbank Avenue, Glasgow 151

Filey 64

Fleming, James 54, 55, 56, 58, 59, 60, 61, 62

Fleming, John 54

Forbes, Inspector 120

Fraser, Kenneth 27

Frederick Street, Glasgow 88
Freemasons 64, 118, 120
Fyne, Loch 90
Gairdner, Dr 67
Galloway 8
Garvie, Max 171–177
Garvie, Sheila 171–177
George Street, Edinburgh 75, 76
Geujan, Margaret 184
Geujan, Thomas 184
Gilchrist, Marion 97–117
Gilmour, Sir John 116
Glasgow 10, 15, 17, 29, 30, 41, 42, 48,
    50, 53, 54, 57, 58, 64, 70, 71, 72, 84,
    87, 88, 98, 106, 127, 156, 157, 158,
    159, 160, 163, 164, 166, 167, 168,
    170, 184, 185
Glasgow Cross 162
Glasgow Fair 83, 87
Glen Sannox 86
Glenboig 168, 170
Glenburn Hydro(pathic) 83, 85
Goatfell 6, 83–89
Goodman, Reverend Gustavus 83, 86
Gosford Bay 179
Grant, Murdoch 24–28
Grant, Robert 26, 27
Grassmarket, Edinburgh 23
grave-robbing 19
Greenock Prison 89
Guibilei, Miss 46
Gulland, Dr Lovell 119
Gunn, Alexander 79, 80, 81
Gunn, Catherine 79
Guthrie, Lord 110, 116
Haddington 179
Haggart, Christina 39
Haldane, Mary 20
Hambrough, Cecil 90–96
Hambrough, Major 91

Hamilton 57, 89
Hamilton Colliery 151
hangings 22, 28, 72, 77, 82, 134, 148,
    156, 183–185
Hare, William 17–23
Higgins, John 132–134
Higgins, Patrick 132–134
Higgins, William 132–134
High Court, Aberdeen 175
High Court, Edinburgh 89, 139
Hill, David 50
Holyroodhouse, Palace of 14, 15
Hope Street, Glasgow 159
Houston, Reverend 153, 154
Huggins and Co. 30, 43, 49
Humanby 64
Hutchinson, Herbert 120
Hutchinson, John 118–123
Hutchison, Charles 118–123
Hutchison, Mrs Charles 118, 119, 120
India Street, Glasgow 35, 103
Invercloy 84, 86
Inverness 28
Ivanhoe 84, 85
James, King 10
James V, King 12
James VI, King 15
James Street, Glasgow 161
Jenkins, Mrs 40, 42, 43
Johnstone, Johnnie 184
Keith, Detective 114
Kenmore 145
Kennedy, T. F. 39
Kenneth the dreamer 27
Kincardineshire 171
King, Jessie 78–82, 185
Kirk o' Field House 16
Kneilands, Anne 150, 154, 155
Knightswood, Glasgow 163
Knox, John 12

Knox, Dr Robert 18, 19, 20, 21, 22
Laing, Detective Inspector John 120
Laird, Margaret 18, 22
Laird, William 49, 50
Lambie, Nellie 98–102, 105, 109, 111–114, 116
Lanarkshire 89, 150, 167
Landressy Street, Glasgow 161
L'Angelier, Pierre Emile 29–53
Langford, Jean 162, 163
Langside, Glasgow 159
Langside Place, Glasgow 159
Laurie, John Watson (John Annandale) 84–89
Lauriston Castle 174
Lindsay, Earl of 14
Linlithgow 85
Lochgilphead 151
Logan, Francis 87
Log's boarding house, Edinburgh 18
London Road, Glasgow 161
Longniddry 179
Longside 147
Lusitania 104, 113
McAdam, Pat 167, 169
MacDonald, Jemima (Mima) 160, 161
McDonald, Mary 55
MacDougal, Anne 21
MacDougal, Helen 18, 21, 22
McGirn, Elizabeth 65, 66
Macintyre, Archie 145
MacIntyre, Catherine 145, 146, 147
Macintyre, Peter 145
MacKeith Street, Glasgow 160, 161
McLachlan, Jessie 54–62
McPherson, Jess 54–62
McLeod, Hugh 24–28
McLeod, Mary 66, 69, 70, 71
McPherson, Jess 54–62
Macpherson, Mrs 79
Maitland, Earl of 16

Majestic Ballroom, Glasgow 159
Manuel, Peter Thomas Anthony 149–156
Marshall Hall, Sir Edward 111
Mary of Guise 12
Mary Queen of Scots 12–16
McClure, A. 107
Merret, Bertha 135–140
Merret, John Donald (Ronald Chesney) 135–144
Merret, Vera (née Isobel Veronica Bonnar) 140, 141, 142, 143
Mickel, Francis 85
Miller, Anthony Joseph 185
Miller, John 184
Milne, Jean 124–131
Minnoch, William 34, 35, 36, 37, 40, 41, 44, 45, 46, 51
Mitchell, Dr 119
Monson, Mr 90–96
Monson, Mrs 91, 93, 95, 96
Moray, James Stewart, Earl of 12, 15
Morton, Earl of 14, 15, 16
Mount Vernon, Glasgow 153
Murdoch Brothers (chemist's) 40
Musselburgh 118, 119, 120
Myszka, Stanislav 145–148
National Trust for Scotland 96
Neuk, The 118–123
Newell, Susan 184
Newington Academy 74
Niddry Mains Farm 133
North British Daily Mail 88
O'Brien, Margaret 160
Ord, Superintendent 114, 115
'ordeal by touch' 26
Orr, Chief Superintendent 113, 114
Paisley 170
Park, William 115
Paterson, Dr James 68, 69, 70

Paterson, Mary 20
Patterson, Mary 69
Pearson, Michael 79, 82
Penn, Mr 139
Penrith 67
Perry, Mary 31, 39, 40, 42, 43, 44
Perth 145, 146, 184
Perth High Court 147
Perth Prison 89, 148
Peterhead 147
Peterhead Prison 89, 110, 150
Peters, Alan 174, 175, 176, 177
Phillpot, Mr 39
Picardy Place, Edinburgh 136
Platt family 152, 153, 154
Portobello, Edinburgh 42
Pritchard, Dr Edward William 63–72
Pritchard, Mary Jane (née Taylor) 64,
    66, 67, 68, 69, 70, 71, 72
Puttock, Helen 161, 162, 163, 164
Rainbow Tavern, Edinburgh 49
Renfield Street, Glasgow 107
Renfrew Street, Glasgow 39
Rhu 31, 32, 45
Rizzio, David 12, 13, 14, 15
Robertson, Elizabeth 185
Robertson, George 185
Rose, Edwin 83–89
Rothesay 83, 87, 88
Roughead, William 63
Royal Crescent, Glasgow 66
Royal Infirmary, Edinburgh 76, 138,
    140
Royal Mile, Edinburgh 178
Ruthven, Lord 14, 15
St George's Road, Glasgow 103
St Mary's Street, Edinburgh 178
Sandyford Place, Glasgow 54, 55, 56,
    58, 59
Sauchiehall Street, Glasgow 30, 40, 66

Schaller, Gerda 142
Scotstoun, Glasgow 161, 163
Scott, Edward 93
Scott, George 136
Scott, Helen 178–182
serial killers 11, 17, 157, 158
Shaughnessy, Mr 111
Sheehy, Lena 53
Sherrin, Mr 119
Simpson, Abigail 19
Slater, Oscar 6, 97–117, 131
Smart family 153, 154, 155
Smith, Bessie 30
Smith, George 29, 30, 31, 35, 36, 38,
    44
Smith, Janet 48
Smith, Madeleine 6, 29–53
Smith, Robert 184
Stephen, Sir Herbert 115
Stevenson, William 43, 53
Stewart, Lord James *see* Moray, James
    Stewart, Earl of
Stirling 41
Stockbridge, Edinburgh 79
Stonehaven 171
Surgeon's Hall, Edinburgh 22
Surgeon's Square, Edinburgh 18
Sutherland 24
Sutherland, Henrietta 137, 139, 140
Sweeney, Edward 93, 94
Tanner's Close, Edinburgh 18, 19, 20, 21
Taylor, Dr 67
Taylor, Mary Jane *see* Pritchard, Mary
    Jane
Taylor, Michael 64
Taylor, Mrs Michael 66, 67, 68, 69, 70,
    71, 72
Taymouth Castle 146
Tevendale, Brian 172, 173, 174, 175,
    176, 177

Thom, William 85
Thuau, Monsieur 43
Tombuie Estate 145
Tomlinson, Violet 80, 81
Torrance, Helen 23
Tower Cottage 145, 146, 147
Towers, Mrs 42
Trench, Detective-Lieutenant John
  Thomson 102, 111–115, 127, 128,
  130, 131
Troup, Alexander 126
Uddingston 153
Ure, Alexander, Lord Advocate 107,
  108, 109, 116
Waldie, Jean 23
Walker, Mrs 84, 86

Wardle, George 53
Warner, Charles 130–131
Waterloo Street, Glasgow 170
Watt, Marion 151
Watt, Vivienne 151
Watt, William 151, 152, 154, 155
West Lothian 132
West Port, Edinburgh 21
West Princes Street, Glasgow 98, 100,
  112
Wood, John 128
Wooley's Tea-room, Invercloy 85
World's End murders 178–182
Young, Alice 166, 167, 169
Young, Thomas Ross 166–170